A Short History of Society

Mary Evans

Open University Press

Open University Press
McGraw-Hill Education
McGraw-Hill House
Shoppenhangers Road
Maidenhead
Berkshire
England
SL6 2QL

email: enquiries@openup.co.uk
world wide web: www.openup.co.uk

and Two Penn Plaza, New York, NY 10121–2289, USA

First published 2006

A catalogue record of this book is available from the British Library.

ISBN–10: 0 335 0335 220 673 (pb) 0335 220681 (hb)
ISBN–13: 978 0335 220 670 (pb) 978 0335 220 687 (hb)

Library of Congress Cataloging-in-Publication Data
CIP data applied for

Typeset by YHT Ltd, London
Printed in Great Britain by Bell & Bain Ltd, Glasgow

A Short History
of Society

Contents

Acknowledgements

I would like to thank a number of people for their help whilst I was working on this book. Chris Cudmore of the Open University Press welcomed the original idea and was an extremely helpful and supportive first reader. Vicky Hall and Gemma Chapman provided invaluable help with the preparation of the manuscript. My sons Tom and Jamie provided their own different contributions on the nature of the modern world and were always interested in the ideas discussed here.

Preface

The cover of this book reproduces *Las Meninas*, painted by the Spanish artist Velazquez in 1656. Far more than any words can convey, this painting suggests much about the world in which we live: our recognition of its diversity and our self-consciousness about our social and personal selves. But given the date of its completion, the painting also suggests the continuities between different epochs: we can recognize ourselves in *Las Meninas* and that should give us some sense that we share a history with the people who lived in the seventeenth century. This book is premised on the importance of that relationship.

Amongst the many important themes of George Orwell's novel *1984* is the way in which highly controlled societies can eliminate history. This book does not argue that the society in which we live has consciously attempted to banish our history and our collective memory of the past; whether or not that has happened is a matter for other discussions. But the following pages are written in the light of the disappearance, in various contexts, of both the chronological teaching of history and the recognition of the importance of the context of ideas and events. We are told that we live in a new 'risk' society (Ulrich Beck) and that human beings and their relationships with each other and themselves are radically different (Anthony Giddens, Bryan Turner and Donna Haraway).[1] All these, and many other writers, offer interpretations of the twenty-first century which emphasize its difference from previous historical periods. This book does not engage with those questions but offers an account of the world before these apparently transforming events and is an attempt to show something of both the interrelationship of ideas and their context and the relationship of the past to the present. There are, however, a number of issues which need to be set out before readers begin this story.

The first is that this book assumes that 'society' exists. The British prime minister Mrs Thatcher famously stated that 'society' did not exist, and various sociologists (for example John Urry) have developed aspects of this idea, arguing that in a global world we no

longer live in disparate societies but in one universe.[2] The appeal of
this idea (in the world after the fall of the Berlin wall in 1989 and the
consequent dissolution of the Soviet Union) is considerable, but in
the view of this author it needs to be resisted, for two reasons. In the
first place, the immediate social world in which we live is an
important part of our identity and we need to understand how that
world has emerged. The second is that the idea that 'history' ended
with the dismantling of the Soviet Empire is one which has been
disowned even by its major protagonist, the writer Francis
Fukuyama.[3] It is evident that the tensions between cultures and
societies which pervade the world today, for example about the
appropriate place of religion in the social world, are part of our
inheritance. The historian Peter Laslett once wrote of 'worlds we
have lost', but another historian, Patrick Collinson, also wrote of our
ability to reclaim, understand and appreciate the importance of
those worlds.[4]

The second set of issues that needs to be addressed briefly here is
that of the terms 'modern', 'modernity' and 'modernism'. These
words are often used as if they had the same meaning, whereas in fact
they can be sharply distinguished. In historical terms the 'modern' is
a movable feast (as Chapter 1 here suggests) but I have taken the term
to apply to the years after 1500, the years in which the Reformation
gave Europe a new version of Christianity: that of Protestantism. The
degree of the impact of that new form of Christianity is a matter of
debate and argument, but no one would deny that this development
mattered, and in many ways continues to matter. The second term,
'modernity', is taken here, as in most other contexts, to apply to that
form of understanding and experience of the world which emerged
in Europe in the mid-nineteenth century. Partly defined by the sense
of change of that period in history, and partly by the new sense of
human possibility that came with it, 'modernity' defines a particular
sense of the social and cultural world. 'Modernism', the third term of
this trio, is used here specifically in the sense of the movement in the
arts which took place in the last years of the nineteenth century and
the first decade of the twentieth.

The major emphasis of this book is on Britain, but Britain's story
is not, we now recognize, a story of one culture or one place. Ideas of
feminism, sexual politics, the 'post-colonial' and 'subaltern studies'
and writers such as Paul Gilroy have all made the writing of history a
more diverse and more richly populated place than it sometimes was
in the past.[5] Thus, whilst Britain is a focus, it is taken for granted that

the realms of the nation were not sealed to ideas from beyond it. The second point here is that readers need to recognize that capitalism and industrialization are not synonymous terms. Capitalism, the political economy of the market and the profit motive, existed long before industrialization and neither depends on the other for its existence. The years after 1989 have done much to 'naturalize' the idea that the market economy is the only way in which societies can be organized (and those years have done quite as much as well to further the idea that democracy and the market economy are 'naturally' linked), but a glance at the past five hundred years would tell us that neither of these ideas is true. Democracy had (and has) to be fought for and defended. If history has any lessons to teach us, it is that there is very little in human affairs that is 'natural'. One final word: the brevity of this account of the past five hundred is such as to exclude, inevitably, many of the events and personalities which have 'made' history. I very much hope that readers will be encouraged to discover more about the making of their past.

Chapter 1

The Making of the Modern

1314   Publication of Dante's *The Divine Comedy*
1492   The 're-conquest' of Granada by Ferdinand and Isabella of
       Spain
       Christopher Columbus arrives in the West Indies
1501   Michelangelo completes work on the statue *David*
1517   Martin Luther's *95 Theses* are published in Wittenberg
1547   The Council of Trent; the beginning of the
       Counter-Reformation
1564   Birth of Shakespeare
1605   Publication of the first volume of *Don Quixote* by Cervantes
1633   Forced repudiation by Galileo of the work of Copernicus

The Europe that confronts us at the beginning of this study is, for
some students of human history, a world which is in certain
important ways definably 'modern'. Yet for many of us, arriving in
Europe in 1500 would be an enormous shock to our twenty-first
century expectations and sensibilities. There would be towns and
cities (and, if we live in some of the older European cities, those
urban spaces would be immediately recognizable), but the people
that we would meet there, and the people that we would be if we
became citizens of the sixteenth century, would be in many respects
different from our modern selves. Few of us now over the age of 50
would be alive; most of us would believe in the explanations given to
us by the Catholic Church about the origin of the world; we would
have little or no control over our own mortality or fertility; and there
is a reasonable chance that we would be both illiterate and often
hungry. Certainly, we would be endlessly concerned about the
availability of food and shelter; we would know that for the great
majority of us old age and infirmity would make us dependent on the
charity of our families or the Church. Despite the best efforts of
Hollywood to make the medieval world look colourful and comfortable, on the whole it was not. Although beautiful buildings were

built, and miracles of craft produced, the general experience of life in the fifteenth century was one of precariousness and uncertainty.

Whether or not this world was 'modern' is a question that has been a matter of some debate. For some historians the modern world does not begin until the French Revolution of 1789; for others the history of 'modern' Europe begins with the Renaissance and the Reformation; yet others date the 'modern' as only properly existing from the beginning of the twentieth century. There is a cluster of dates towards the end of the fifteenth century which have sometimes been taken as the date of the beginning of the 'modern': for example, 1492 and the first voyage of Christopher Columbus (1451–1506) to the New World, 1501 and the completion by Michelangelo (1475–1564) of work on the statue *David*, or 1485 and the end, in England, of the Wars of the Roses. All these dates are taken as indicative of the coming of the modern in that they herald new departures in the social world. An alternative account of the modern suggests that it was in the fourteenth, rather than in the sixteenth, century that certain characteristics emerged in European society which indicate a shift towards 'modern' ways of thinking and of understanding the world. Certainly, by 1500 the nature of the physical relationship between Europe and the rest of the world had been enlarged by the voyage of Christopher Columbus to the West Indies and what used to be described as the 'discovery' of the 'New World'. By this time, too, the first travel book had been written (by Abu Abdallah Muhammad Ibn Battutah, who was born in Tangier in 1304 and whose book, entitled *Travels*, was published in the 1350s). What that book showed was that the links between distant cultures existed long before those more commonly cited 'years of exploration' in the sixteenth and seventeenth centuries. Indeed, the world of Ibn Battutah was extensive, a world united by trade and Islam, which stretched from Bengal to North Africa and united parts of East Africa with the southern slopes of the Himalayas. Marco Polo is often cited as the first great European traveller, but Ibn Battutah, although he began his journeys after Polo's death, was an even more assiduous traveller. For those millions of citizens who barely travelled to the next village, these journeys, if known at all, existed only as stories about a distant world. The great travellers of the fourteenth century wrote down accounts of their journeys, but for the largely illiterate population of Europe in the fourteenth century their stories were part of an oral tradition. Nevertheless, the world was becoming ever smaller, even if for most of the population of Europe at this time the known world had entirely local boundaries.

This example of the travels of fourteenth-century individuals is used to illustrate the ways in which it is possible to support that case for regarding the fourteenth century as the century in which 'the modern' begins. Historical periodization is always complex and unsatisfactory, but if we take as characteristic of the modern a sense of the importance of individual experience, there is much in Europe of the fourteenth century to suggest that it is in this century that we can find the emergence of our 'modern' selves. But this would be a judgement which prioritizes the cultural above the medical, scientific and the technological: we can point to the emergence of narrative about recognizable, 'ordinary' human beings (Chaucer and Dante, both writing in the fourteenth century), claims for religious and political democracy (the Lollards, the followers of John Wycliffe), the development or establishment of many famous European universities (at Coimbra, Paris, Oxford, Cambridge and Bologna) and humanist optimism about the possibilities of the human condition. But at the same time we have to recognize a society that was still subject to the ravages and the demands of nature. Indeed, the Black Death of 1348–49 had wiped out about one-third of the population of Europe and the fate of many millions lay on the success or failure of each year's harvest. The 'modern' people of the fourteenth century may have travelled widely and written with timeless sympathy of human emotions, but they were still locked into a perilous relationship with the natural world. In other ways too, notably the unity of Christendom, their world was not modern in the sense that we have come to understand the word. So, whilst the fourteenth century contains much that is familiar to us, this text will begin with the first years of the sixteenth century.

These introductory remarks are – as is this text – about the history of British society, the changing contours of that society and others in Europe, and the relationship of those societies with the rest of the world. But, as the above suggests, this is not a text which sees Britain, or Europe, as a sealed and fortress-like geographical and cultural area, which neither knew or was unfamiliar to other cultures. Human curiosity and human greed has always ensured that cultures and societies intermix, in ways that are either blatantly aggressive or rather more peaceful. The history of Europe up to the beginning of the sixteenth century would suggest that it was largely the former type of relationship that predominated: many histories speak of the

Norman 'Conquest', the Viking 'invasions' and the 'Wars of the Roses'. But out of these various military exploits had emerged, by the end of the fifteenth century, many of the recognizable nation states of modern Europe such as France, Portugal, Hungary, Poland, Spain (after the marriage of Ferdinand of Aragon and Isabella of Castile) and England had achieved something like their modern boundaries. Other European societies existed as independent city states (Italy) or principalities (Italy and Germany) but united by common languages. More than any unity of language however, was the unity of Europe – until the Reformation – in allegiance to the Catholic Church, an allegiance cemented by two essential beliefs: belief in the Mass and belief in the religious supremacy of the Pope. If the religious supremacy of the Pope had sometimes been strained (by the existence of two, and, at one time, three Popes in the schisms that occurred between 1378 and 1449), the belief in the Mass was a central unifying force in Europe and was, in the sixteenth century, to be the issue which tore Europe apart.

The word 'Mass' is a western nickname for the central act of faith of the Christian Church. Emerging out of the depiction of the Last Supper on the night before the crucifixion of Jesus Christ, the Mass, or Eucharist, is an abbreviated account of Christian beliefs about the relationship of God to the world. Bread and wine, everyday parts of life, through the doctrine of transubstantiation became transformed in the Mass to the body and blood of Jesus Christ. Belief created eternal life out of the everyday participation in this ritual and gave to believers an affirmation of life after death. The considerable consolation offered by this idea to the many people of the fourteenth and fifteenth centuries whose lives on earth were likely to be brief was no doubt part of its appeal. However, Christianity was very much more than a religion which gave support to people whose lives were hard and arduous: it was the inspiration not only for acts of extreme violence against other religions (and in England the first ever expulsion of the Jews from a particular state by Edward I) but also for the Gothic masterpieces of art and architecture which became part of the European landscape. In addition, it is often supposed that work regulated other than by the natural pattern of daylight did not become part of European experience until the days of the factory system and the Industrial Revolution. Anyone living in a Benedictine or Cistercian monastery in the thirteenth or fourteenth century would have found this idea ludicrous, since those institutions had finely developed and regulated patterns of work, sleep and prayer.

Within these institutions, the German sociologist Max Weber (1864–1920) was to argue, lay some of the seeds of the later remarkable technological and intellectual developments of the sixteenth century.

Europe in the years before the beginning of the sixteenth century was, perhaps, more united than at any other time in its history, and the cultural force behind this unity was that of Christianity. What Europe also shared at this time was the common experience of being an agricultural society: the vast majority of people lived and worked on the land, seldom left it and had little experience of what we now take for granted as urban life. But part of the importance of the fourteenth century as a transitional point in European history was the collapse, after the Black Death, of the feudal system and the emergence of what we now know as wage labour. Slavery and serfdom certainly persisted in parts of Europe, but by the sixteenth century many people shared the recognizably modern experience of earning a living by selling their labour rather than performing – as in serfdom – unpaid labour for a feudal lord. This transformation of social relations is a crucial part of the emergence of the modern world: it was a transformation which reorganized the social distribution of power, the meaning of the law and the eventual emergence of the idea of the formally free citizen with social rights and responsibilities. It was still the case – and was to remain so for several centuries – that men were considered to be the definitive form of human being, from whom women were, in the words of the Bible, 'Adam's Rib' and both an inferior form of the male and responsible for Man's fall from grace in the Garden of Eden. But European society did not enforce either rigid patterns of sexual segregation or refuse to allow women, should they be rich enough or determined enough, to participate in both political and cultural life. Women rulers, women members of religious communities and many anonymous women played their part in the events and the culture that shaped European societies in the years before the Reformation.[1]

It was in the early fifteenth century that there occurred a technological revolution, which was to help to shatter the religious hegemony of Europe and to provide for its people a step towards ideas of democracy and citizenship. That revolution was the introduction of printing, or, more precisely, the generalized use of movable type. Amongst historians of the fifteenth and sixteenth centuries there appears to be a consensus that, in the words of Diarmaid MacCulloch, 'the coming of printing changed the shape of religion'.[2] For MacCulloch, and others, the availability of Bibles helped to create the Reformation, but if this was not enough, it was also the case that the effect of printing was to change Europe's ideas about knowledge and the originality of thought. Those busy – and well-organized – monks in the monasteries of the thirteenth and fourteenth centuries might have assumed that 'writing' was literally that; it was not until the invention of printing that 'writing' could begin to take on our modern understanding of the term which assumes that 'writing' involves a creative process quite as much as the activity of the scribe. No longer, once printing existed, could ideas be 'owned' by that tiny number of people with the resources to buy and store expensive manuscripts. Now any idea, any text, could be, as the great German sociologist Walter Benjamin was to describe it some four hundred years later, 'mechanically reproduced'.[3] Yet at the same time we need to recognize that dissenting ideas existed prior to the invention of printing, although circulated through manuscripts and oral discussion.

The coming of the technology of printing has sometimes been regarded as the first great democratic revolution of the modern world. That judgement emphasizes the inherent challenge to authority that printing represents: as repressive regimes have always recognized, words do matter, and a technology that allows potentially dangerous ideas to be widely distributed is not one that is necessarily welcome. By the end of the sixteenth century there must have been many European princes and prelates who wished that printing had never become widely available, since the social movement which was printing's first legacy to the world was the Reformation: the successful challenge to the religious authority of the Catholic Church and the event whose ramifications continue to structure the world in which we live. For anyone interested in the nature of the contemporary world, the Reformation is the event that probably more than any other shaped many of the fundamental patterns of the ideas and the assumptions by which we live. Indeed, for many sociologists, and in particular for Max Weber, the Reformation produced what he famously described (in the book of the same title) as the guiding ethos of the modern world: 'the Protestant ethic and the spirit of capitalism'.[4]

The Protestant Reformation had its origins in discontents in the early sixteenth century within the Catholic Church. For centuries there had been disagreements and tensions within the Catholic Church (for example between those sympathetic to the teaching of

Aristotle and those more sympathetic to that of St Augustine); dogma and doctrine were not static and the Pope was not given absolute religious authority until the nineteenth century. But what was expected of the Church, in this era before the emergence of modern science, was that it would explain the world and provide an account of both its origins and its proper order. The challenge to this assumption came from various quarters across Europe, most famously perhaps the *95 Theses* of Martin Luther, reputedly nailed to a church door in Wittenberg on 31 October 1517. (This date has been celebrated in some German-speaking lands as Reformation Day). At the heart of Luther's challenge to the Pope on this occasion was the issue of indulgences (the sale of forgiveness to those who had sinned), but this issue was only part of the more fundamental question of faith and its role in religion and religious practice. For Luther and his contemporaries – the Frenchman John Calvin (1509–64) author of *Institutes of the Christian Religion* (1535), the Swiss Huldrych Zwingli (1484–1531) and the English Thomas Cranmer (1489–1556) – what differentiated their position on Christian faith from that of the Catholic Church was that of their understanding of the fall of Man: for Luther and Calvin in particular, the only possible route to human redemption lay through faith; there was no space for human agency in the repair of this situation. (Zwingli also took the view that Luther was too close to the Catholics in his view of Christ's humanity.) Since this view arguably challenged the idea that the Christian God had given men free will, Luther's views were not universally accepted. Most prominent – and of most lasting fame – amongst those who resisted Luther was Desiderius Erasmus (1466–1536), who found Luther's views unacceptable on the profoundly modern grounds that Luther did not allow for the capacity of human beings for 'reason'.

Pope Leo X excommunicated Luther in 1520 and rulers throughout Europe burnt Luther's now widely available books and issued proclamations against heresy. Amongst those rulers who energetically fought for the Pope at this time was England's Henry VIII, whose efforts on the Pope's behalf earned him the title 'Defender of the Faith'. But despite these efforts, the ideas of Luther and others began to take hold with significant numbers of the clergy and of the laity. One of the great attractions for the clergy was that Luther was quite prepared to countenance the marriage of the priesthood; for the laity the attraction of Luther's ideas was complex, but not least amongst the attraction for German-speaking populations was the idea of a religion independent of the control of Rome. What we can see at work here is the emergent strength of national identity; an identity which goes beyond that of locality and is much enhanced by the experience of a shared written language, a written language which is increasingly available to all. This idea was not lost on Henry VIII who ordered, in 1537, that all English parish churches should be provided with English translations of the Bible. (It is also important to point out that Henry became somewhat alarmed by the social implications of this idea and in 1543 persuaded Parliament to pass a law stating that only people of higher social status should be allowed to read the Bible.)

Religious dissent and disagreement in the years after Luther's excommunication in 1520 was to take the form in Europe of bloody and destructive civil and national wars. By the end of the sixteenth century the religious allegiances of Europe had divided the continent, very approximately, into the Catholic south and the Protestant north. 'Protestantism' had become part of European experience and history, and with it, sociologists and cultural historians have long supposed, had come a radically different way of understanding the world and behaving within it. But that radically different way of looking at the world had not come only from changes in religion, it had also emerged from the other great cultural event that is associated with the fourteenth, fifteenth and sixteenth centuries: the Renaissance. The history of this idea is in some ways rather more complex – and contentious – than that of the Reformation, since there is no date in the Renaissance to match the historical certainty of Luther's *95 Theses* or the Act of Supremacy of 1531, which made Henry VIII supreme head of the Church of England. The history of the very idea of the Renaissance shows how much interpretations of the past have changed in the twentieth century: the first major historian of the Renaissance, and the person to invent the term, was the French historian Jules Michelet, who wrote in 1855 that the Renaissance meant 'the discovery of the world and the discovery of man', an idea which very clearly defined the Renaissance in terms of the emergence of humanism in Europe in the fourteenth and fifteenth centuries.[5] Michelet, himself deeply committed to the egalitarian ideas of the French Revolution, argued that the Renaissance was about the specifically modern ideas of individuals such as Michelangelo (1475–1564), Montaigne (1533–92), Shakespeare (1564–1616) and Galileo (1564–1642). The next great historian of the Renaissance, the Swiss academic Jacob Burckhardt, was to make the

Renaissance specifically Italian. In *The Civilization of the Renaissance in Italy* (published in 1860), Burckhardt celebrated the 'modern spirit', which separated the people of the Renaissance from what he clearly regarded as the dark ages of medieval Europe.[6] The third great nineteenth-century historian of the Renaissance, the Englishman Walter Pater, extended the historical boundaries of the Renaissance from the twelfth to the seventeenth century and celebrated what he saw as the love of imagination and the senses which Renaissance artists evoked.[7]

Twentieth-century accounts of the Renaissance have challenged many of the assumptions of nineteenth-century critics. Johan Huizinga's *The Waning of the Middle Ages* (published in 1919) took issue with the idea of sharp divisions between the Renaissance and the Middle Ages and with the refusal to recognize the achievements of countries other than Italy.[8] But perhaps more influential, and important for all students of cultural life and cultural change, was Erwin Panofsky's *Studies in Iconology* (published in 1939), which claimed that the study and the interpretation of art is a measure of our humanity.[9] For Panofsky, Renaissance art is the pinnacle of human achievement, the moment when people came to understand the nature of their humanity. Accounts in the later part of the twentieth century have returned (for example in the work of Stephen Greenblatt) to the idea of the Renaissance as the cradle of the modern, the point at which people begin to practise what Greenblatt describes as 'self-fashioning'.[10] Whatever the account of the Renaissance that we find the most convincing, what is apparent from all of them is that by the end of the sixteenth century the cultural map of Europe had shifted to allow hugely expanded possibilities for individual scepticism, authorship and creativity.

The museums and art galleries of Europe (and indeed the rest of the world) are replete with the various extraordinary achievements of what is known, however loosely and with however much contention, as the Renaissance. Visitors to those museums in the twenty-first century, in much the same way as visitors to the great cathedrals of Europe, see the artefacts in contexts which minimize their social origins and the values attached to them. What needs to be emphasized here is that although there is a degree of critical consensus about the Renaissance as the period in which the 'modern' began, many of the great works of the period were inspired by religious commitments and allegiances. The claiming of Leonardo da Vinci (1452–1519), Michelangelo or Shakespeare for 'the modern' is in certain ways perfectly appropriate, if we assume that the 'modern' includes a respect and admiration for the individual. But at the same time, the assumption that the modern is by definition secular, and that the great figures of Renaissance art and literature can be claimed for a secular tradition, is a more problematic idea.

On this issue of the centrality of religion to the history of the fifteenth and sixteenth centuries it is useful to return to Max Weber. But it is also important to note that Weber, in common with Karl Marx and those cultural historians of the Renaissance mentioned above, had a profound interest in the past as part of an understanding of the present. A feature of the 'making' of modern society, and the study of modern society, has thus been, at least in the nineteenth and twentieth centuries, a consistent concern with the origins of ideas and values. Across disciplines in the social sciences and the humanities there has been a sense of the importance of understanding the past, an importance which is particularly well illustrated in what is known as the 'classic' tradition in sociology. The three key figures who make up this tradition, Karl Marx (1818–83), Max Weber and Emile Durkheim (1858–1917), all interrogated ideas about the modern and tried to offer accounts of how those ideas, said to be characteristic of the modern, emerged. What all three emphasize is the key question of the relation between changes in ideas and material changes, an idea which Weber was to pursue in his study of the Reformation.

Unlike cultural historians, for whom the Renaissance is the key cultural transformation of fifteenth- and sixteenth-century Europe, for Weber the crucial event is the Reformation. Weber notes, in *The Protestant Ethic and the Spirit of Capitalism*, that capitalism in the sixteenth century seemed to be associated with Protestant Europe and Protestant individuals. But, as Weber recognized, the conditions for capitalism (a money economy, banking, trading and technological competence and innovation) existed in various societies throughout Europe (and indeed the world) and yet those societies had not become capitalist. Weber's thesis was that those arguments put by Luther and others which led to the articulation of a specifically Protestant form of Christianity were arguments which also underpinned the development of a mindset which valued secular success and the pursuit of profit. It is the thesis about the pursuit of profit which is crucial here; Weber (and Marx) knew perfectly well that the human desire to accumulate is ancient. But what they both suggested is that the desire to accumulate for its own sake is the significant difference between capitalist Europe (the Europe which emerges in the sixteenth century) and pre-capitalist Europe.

It is here, then, that we have another interpretation, and indeed another emphasis, about the changes that took place in Europe in the sixteenth century. On the one hand are those historians who see the century as the point at which 'modern' understanding and behaviour began to be formed, whereas for others the meaning of the new behaviour was certainly a new way of looking at the world, which was that of the 'Protestant ethic'. These ideas are not, of course, binary opposites, and rigid lines cannot be drawn between different kinds of changes. Indeed, as much as Weber argued that the values of many people did change in the sixteenth century, there are others who saw little or no shift in values or behaviour.[11] Yet what Weber saw as the inherent psychic loneliness of Protestantism is perhaps the most striking feature of his thesis: the refusal of Calvin's theology to offer any consolation to human beings about the possibility of their salvation and the complete condemnation by Calvinism of any form of hedonism or idleness. Weber wrote thus:

> In its extreme inhumanity this doctrine must above all have had one consequence for the life of a generation which surrendered to its magnificent consistency. That was a feeling of unprecedented inner loneliness of the single individual. In what was for the man of the age of the Reformation the most important thing in life, his eternal salvation, he was forced to follow his path alone to meet a destiny which had been decreed for him from eternity. No one could help him.[12]

It is in this theology that lay (apart from the appalling fear of not being saved) the refusal of many Protestant churches to countenance religious art and the Puritan distaste for personal display or adornment. What Protestantism thus came to be associated with was the fervent belief in hard work as a form of religious salvation; in centuries after the sixteenth the idea was to be secularized so that belief in hard work became a value in itself, quite apart from any religious associations.

The tensions that were created in sixteenth-century Europe as a result of the Reformation were immense: it is no exaggeration to say that the Reformation created religious wars in a continent which had previously kept battles about religion to engagements outside

Europe. An important part of what occurred as a result of religious conflict was the reawakening of intolerance towards other religions: Europe in the sixteenth century saw certain revivals of anti-Semitism and a heightened sense of the difference between Christian Europe and Islamic societies. It is not the case that the Reformation can be blamed for all such manifestations of intolerance: for example, the expulsion of the Moors from Granada in Spain in 1492 pre-dated the emergence of Protestantism and had as much to do with a sense of territorial ownership as it did with religion. But that example serves to illustrate the ways in which ideas about religion and ideas about nation became so deeply entwined in sixteenth-century Europe. Historians are generally sceptical about using the idea of nationalism in the context of fifteenth- and sixteenth-century Europe, arguing that the concept cannot be used with any reliability until after 1789 and the emergence of countries with consolidated territory, a single language and a common culture. (In the England of the fifteenth century, for example, there were five different spoken languages: English, Welsh, Cornish, Manx and French). Nevertheless, what we can observe in some European states (countries with recognizably 'modern' contours such as England or Portugal) was a sense of loyalty to the national (be it a dynasty such as the Tudors) or a local guild or corporation. The loyalties articulated by a sense of belonging to these groups did create an antagonism to demands by others – outsiders – for fealty. England is the best example of a sixteenth-century state whose sense of national identity was created less by internal cohesion than by external threat. Indeed, the forging of the state religion of England, the Church of England, was born out of this desire for national rather than foreign control of religion.

But in that account of the making of Anglicanism there lies many instances of what Weber was to describe as the 'unintended consequences' of human action. Weber's view of the Reformation, and the emergence of ascetic Protestantism, is that its prime mover was John Calvin; the other three most important forms of worldly asceticism were Pietism, Methodism and the sects growing out of the Baptist movement.[13] Luther, as far as anyone can judge, had no more wish than Henry VIII to cause schism in Christendom and most historians of Tudor England point to the continuing allegiance of Henry VIII to the beliefs and teaching of the Catholic Church. Henry himself was no religious radical, but what he did want was a male heir for the throne of England. Refused permission to annul his first marriage to Catherine of Aragon, Henry (aided and abetted by

Thomas Cromwell) came to the conclusion that the only way through his difficulties (and to be free to marry Anne Boleyn) was to reject the authority of the Pope. It was thus that Henry made himself supreme head of the Church of England and established in England a unique alliance between religion and nation. But this was not in itself a commitment to Protestantism as defined by Luther, let alone Calvin. The making of the 'spirit of capitalism' was to evolve after Henry VIII's break with Rome and the greater influence, in the late sixteenth and early seventeenth centuries of ascetic Protestantism.

The Pope (Clement VII) might well have felt more sympathetic to Henry had not the English proved to be unhelpful in the defence of Europe against the Turks and if Catherine of Aragon's family had not had considerable control over the Papacy. But what the case of Henry VIII's complex divorce proceedings illustrate is the tangled web of alliances, loyalties, competing motivations and unforeseen events, which led to the final resolution of Henry's determined bid for independence from the papacy. Henry achieved want he wanted, in that he married Anne Boleyn. But as we know, and he did not at the time, the longed-for child born of this marriage would be a girl and not a boy. The laws of patriarchal inheritance being what they were (and are) in England, the birth of a girl was of little consolation to Henry. The problems of the Tudor succession were thus not solved by a break with Rome, but what Henry had done was to set the scene in England for a long history of anti-Catholic legislation and feeling which was to continue until the twentieth century, and indeed was to have a crucial impact on Anglo-Irish relations.

Other European states in the sixteenth century did not face the particular problems of succession faced by Henry VIII, but what was inescapable in all parts of Europe at that time was the seismic effect of the Reformation on social life and social stability. From the standpoint of the secular West in the twenty-first century, it is sometimes difficult to appreciate fully the deep and passionate commitment that people in the sixteenth century had to religion and to different interpretations of religion. People were prepared to die appalling deaths (and indeed put others to appalling deaths) in defence of different liturgies, of different ways of celebrating Mass and of other matters of church organization. Thomas More (1478–1535), the author of *Utopia* and a friend of Erasmus, is one of the most famous Catholic martyrs of religious dissent and conflict in England, but there were many other, less famous people equally prepared to give up their lives for matters that secular societies might well regard as trivial or as only a matter of private conscience. Two of the three children of Henry VIII, Mary Tudor and Edward VI, took determined views about the matter of religion; their views share the belief of other European states of the sixteenth century in the dictum of 'cuius regio eius religio', essentially the religion of the king is the religion of the country. First proposed at the Diet of Speyer of 1526, the principle was devised to lessen the strife in the German principalities, some supporting Luther and others rejecting him. Rather than allow endless warfare, rulers accepted religious divisions, and by implication the division of Europe into Protestant and Catholic. Only Elizabeth I of England, the half-sister of Edward and Mary, took the recognizably modern view of religion when she said (albeit allegedly) that she 'did not propose to look into men's souls'.

Elizabeth I might have viewed religious belief as a matter of individual conscience (and her view was shared by other rulers, notably Henry IV of France who is famous for remarking that 'Paris is worth a Mass'), but many others in the sixteenth century did not. Notable amongst this group was the Catholic Church, which launched, from the days of the first session of the Council of Trent in 1547, a determined onslaught on the 'heresy' of Protestant teaching. Amongst the most fervent Catholic rulers was Philip II of Spain, who saw (as did his one-time wife Mary Tudor) the reclaiming of Protestant lands as the mission of a good Catholic king. The prosecution of this idea was made possible – be it in Spain, or the Netherlands or in England – by the authority that sixteenth-century rulers possessed over their subjects. Although certain basic rights of citizenship had been established (for example, habeas corpus in England), rulers still had considerable powers to impose their own views on individuals. Yet what was characteristic of many religious prosecutions of the sixteenth century was that they did not involve the immediate progress of the accused to the scaffold or the pyre but were preceded by a form of trial. If this trial, for example the trial of Thomas More in the reign of Henry VIII, involved a person of note, then the courts gave some space for arguments for both the defence and the prosecution. Other trials, notably of those accused of heresy in lands under the jurisdiction of Spain, were little more than the familiar 'show trials' of the twentieth century.

Thus the picture of relations between citizen and state in Europe in the sixteenth century is not one of the absolute autocracy of the ruler and the absolute obedience of subjects. In many European countries, rulers themselves had only achieved power through various kinds of dynastic wars between sections of the nobility; when authority and kingship had been gained by violence it was just as likely that it could be taken away by the same means. Nevertheless, it was not until the power of the European monarchs was finally ended (and the beheading of Louis XVI in 1793 marks that turning point) that European citizens could assume that political power was to take the form of the power of the state. In this respect, therefore, the sixteenth century remains conspicuously 'unmodern' in that one individual, in power through a principle of hereditary right, was able to exercise unique and often unchallenged powers. But at the same time, as many sociologists and political historians have noted, the countries of Europe did not contain the kind of absolute authority that was to be found in other parts of the world. One unhappy consequence for many non-European societies of this difference was that European conquest was much facilitated by the centralization of power in one person in the invaded or colonized state: the destruction of that person essentially involved the destruction of that state.

European monarchs in the sixteenth century, however, had to take cognizance not just of the ambitions of sections of the nobility but also of those parts of society crucial to the maintenance of the economic welfare of the state. Throughout recorded history, states have extracted money from their citizens, in the form of taxes, forced 'gifts' and fines. From the sixteenth century onwards this issue began to figure prominently in the social tensions of Europe and what we see in these years is a beginning of that sense of the necessary negotiation of taxation that was to be so important later in history. (But the absence of money to pay armies often had the positive effect of ending wars and armed conflict: the Peace of Cateau-Cambresis in 1559 between France and Spain is often judged to be a result of the lack of funds of both sides.) The collapse of feudal power meant that the state had to pay its armies; warfare to protect religious views, trading interests and territorial claims was expensive and had to be paid for. Thus various social and occupational groups, guilds, city corporations and the prominent citizens of towns, began to be part of the political order and expected to have their views taken into consideration. Monarchs could acquire funds through what was essentially licensed piracy (Sir Francis Drake was regarded with favour at the Elizabethan court both for his part in the defeat of the Spanish Armada and for his capture of richly laden Spanish galleons) and these funds would pass directly to the central exchequer. But other than this source of money – always unreliable and of course just as likely to result in the loss of treasure as in the gain of some-body else's – monarchs had to raise money in the more orthodox way of taxation, for which they now needed consensus and permission.

The societies from which sixteenth-century monarchs could raise funds were, in many parts of Europe, relatively rich. Although all parts of Europe were, at this point in their history, still dependent on the vagaries of natural forces for next year's survival, many European countries were able to produce considerable amounts of foods and other commodities. Sixteenth-century recipe books attest to the variety of food available (if not to all sections of society) and greater, and more reliable, trade with societies outside Europe had made available new kinds of foods and spices. Eating well, rather than simply eating, acquired a social value; monarchs took their cooks with them when they moved around. Most famously, Catherine de Medici reputedly so mistrusted the food in France that when she began to live there she imported Italian cooks and the Italian refinement of using a fork. This domestic change in the sixteenth century is very much part of what the sociologist Norbert Elias has described as the 'civilizing process', a process which can be observed from the sixteenth century onwards and which involves various forms of social regulation, notably in ways which involve the regulation of the relationship between the body and the social world.[14] The fork may seem like a simple, everyday example of this change, but it is an important part of a shift towards that consciousness of self which is part of modern subjectivity and a sense of self. Sixteenth-century England has been noted for the emergence of etiquette books and the coming of ideas about behaviour which applied to all sections of society, rather than that minority schooled in chivalry and the manners of that 'very gentil, parfait knight' of Chaucer's *Prologue.*

By the end of the sixteenth century the Europe which at the beginning of the century had been united in a common form of Christianity was radically disunited by divergent forms of that religion. The continent had still not taken that leap to the secular which was to be part of the eighteenth and nineteenth centuries, but what had emerged was the sense that the population as a whole had a right to examine the major tenets of religion. The decision by Edward VI of England to make it mandatory for all churches to make available a copy of the Bible in English was a major step towards the democratization of knowledge and the emergence in England, in the seventeenth century, of numerous Protestant sects. England became, after the various troubles of Henry VIII, a Protestant country, albeit a

Protestant country whose state religion contained aspects of belief (for example 'the communion of saints'), which were recognizably Catholic rather than Protestant. Since England effectively marginalized Catholics (and indeed persecuted them in the reign of Edward VI), the country was never to see that flowering of art which was part of the Catholic Counter-Reformation. The centrality of religious figures and themes in painting and the Baroque in architecture were to be features of Catholic, rather than Protestant, Europe. But what England did have, in the late sixteenth century, was the emergence of a confident and assertive national voice in the form of its playwrights, most famously Christopher Marlowe (1564–93) and William Shakespeare. In the works of these men lay the emergence of the vernacular, in terms of language, subject matter and character, in drama. England cannot lay claim to the first novel in European history (Cervantes' *Don Quixote* is the first, and for many people the greatest, European novel) but it can claim a drama, which was both popular (in terms of audience) and accessible. Court patronage played the supportive part of the patronage of the arts that it had always played and was to continue to play until patronage passed from individuals to corporations.

By 1600, bitter civil wars had wrecked parts of Europe and were to continue to do so until the end of the seventeenth century. But the continent was not always at war. Indeed, for many citizens of sixteenth-century Europe the century brought new prosperity and new opportunities: existing trade with countries outside Europe increased and the vast amounts of wealth variously plundered from other societies (notably by Spain from countries of Central and South America) gave employment to many. Governments constantly ran out of money, but individual fortunes were made for a minority of the population. Domestic life for some people became more comfortable as houses acquired fireplaces, windows with glass and wooden floors. The rich no longer built themselves houses as fortresses but began to establish the grand country houses which were to become a feature of the European landscape. Rich men, and occasionally rich women, continued to demonstrate wealth and breeding through the possession of domestic artefacts and beautiful homes. Often regarded as a century which turned with enthusiasm to the idea of 'civilization', we might also regard the sixteenth century as one which began to turn with equal enthusiasm towards the domestic space. That domestic space was, for any household with even a modicum of wealth, one which was well provided with servants: for the wealthy the running of a large house involved scores of people to assist in its upkeep.[15]

The Europe transformed by the religious conflicts of the Reformation is part of a world which stands between the Middle Ages and the emergence in the eighteenth century of a definably 'modern' selfhood, a selfhood which assumes that the proper task of the modern person is to carry forward the rational control of the world in which they live, through the ability both to understand that world and to assume power over it. For the truly 'modern' to emerge it is therefore necessary for us to find in the social world evidence that human beings are thinking about the ways in which society can be run and ordered, rather than assuming that the way in which society is run, at any point in time, is the way in which society should be run. In the seventeenth century, most obviously in England, the 'natural' right of the monarch to rule was challenged by those who took a very different view. James I of England may have defended the Divine Right of Kings, but he did so in the face of the rapidly emerging consensus that the wisdom of the Almighty did not necessarily extend to the appointment of individual rulers. But people in the sixteenth century did not, on the whole, accept this view and to this extent, therefore, we can find in the sixteenth century a very real continuity with the past, rather than the future, of European society. Shakespeare 'humanized' monarchs, in that he made them jealous, angry, ambitious, wasteful and even occasionally magnificent, but the monarch still had a right to rule and, if challenged, was to be challenged by his peers rather than the population as a whole. The idea of democracy, in the sense of a formal right for all to participate in government, was a very long way away in the sixteenth century. Advice books were written for rulers (Niccolò Machiavelli (1469–1527) and the twelfth-century Gerald of Wales being notable authors of this genre), but the assumption in both cases was that the ruler should be instructed in order to be a better (or more effective) ruler rather than one who needed instruction in power sharing.

In another sense too, the sixteenth century is part of the Middle Ages rather than the modern Europe of the twenty-first century. That sense is the sense of themselves which individuals had, in terms of their understanding both of their bodies and of their psyches. The sixteenth century (to judge from Shakespeare and others) had a very full understanding of human motivation but what it did not have, and which marks the century off from our own times, is a modern understanding of the body. This is not to say that people in the sixteenth century did not recognize biological difference or were incapable of knowing and expressing erotic love between individuals; both these capacities were, and always have been, part of the European human condition. The difference is rather that the human body was assumed to be male (women were an aberration from this human 'norm') and that it was rather less subject to the many controls and internalized expectations which have emerged since the eighteenth century, although all communities policed the personal behaviour of their members. Sexual desire was assumed to be part of the world of both sexes: 'For what offence have I, this fortnight been, a banished woman from my husband's bed', asks the wife of Henry IV in Shakespeare's play, and in doing so stakes a claim for the sexual rights of wives which was to disappear in later centuries.

Max Weber claimed that the fissures of the Reformation unleashed in Europe critical and creative powers which already existed. He did not take the view, any more than modern historians or social scientists do, that the sixteenth century was a break with the past or the beginning of the present. But he did argue that what religious transformation encouraged, albeit implicitly, was the sense of the possible transformative power of ideas. In the sixteenth century, we should note, the Catholic Church embraced the idea of banning certain books: this is a truly notable idea in human history since it speaks to the recognition of the availability of books, but even more importantly it recognizes the power of the written word to determine human action. The general *Index* of forbidden books issued in Rome in 1557 by Pope Paul IV was not the first time that books had been banned (in the sixteenth century this had already occurred in Paris, Venice and Henry VIII's England), but it was the first time that a comprehensive and potentially enforceable list had been published. The key works that appeared on the *Index* were obvious candidates such as the works of Luther; less obvious candidates were the entire works of Erasmus and any copy of the Bible in a vernacular language. At the beginning of the seventeenth century, Pope Paul V was entirely serious when he railed at the Venetian ambassador, 'Don't you know that so much reading of Scripture ruins the Catholic religion?' (As a result of views such as these no Italian version of the Bible was published in the Italian peninsula between 1567 and 1773.) The very acute sense of the power of ideas to transform behaviour was clearly not lost on the Vatican.

But even though the acceptance of the modern European idea of tolerating difference was to take at least another two hundred years to become a more commonplace, if fragile, part of European experience, the religious transformations of the Reformation had set in train a shift towards the secular and the loss of authority of the religious. Weber's view was that what had taken place in the Protestant Reformation was the transposition of the religious goal of salvation into the secular goal of success, which included the pursuit of profit. That profit was then to be reinvested rather than spent on consumption or display. In all, what Weber saw as definitive about capitalism, and its emergence in sixteenth-century Europe, was its disciplined, methodical and rule-bound conduct, a view which Weber defined in these terms: 'Be prudent, diligent, and ever about your lawful business; do not idle, for time is money, ... be frugal in consumption and do not waste money on inessentials; and finally, do not let money lie idle, for the smallest sum soundly invested can earn a profit, and the profits reinvested soon multiply in ever increasing amounts.'[16] By the end of the sixteenth century, the Dutch, the English and many parts of northern Germany had begun to take this advice to heart: the Protestant ethic had arrived in northern Europe and was to make of these societies rich trading nations. Spain and Italy, by contrast, were to lose the political and cultural dominance which had been theirs at the beginning of the sixteenth century. For example, Philip II of Spain, king of a vast overseas empire and of a country awash with the riches of the Americas, spectacularly failed to follow Protestant strictures: huge amounts of money arrived in Seville and were spent, but seldom invested.

The craving to see God in a clearer light, and to forge a religion without abuse or flagrant corruption was the setting for the Reformation and for the divisions that emerged in sixteenth-century Europe. At the same time this urgent wish to understand religion more clearly was to become part of the European culture which in the seventeenth century fuelled interest in science and technology and initiated those enquiries in philosophy and political science which heralded the Enlightenment. Thomas Hobbes, John Locke and René Descartes, early figures of the European Enlightenment were motivated by the same wish to clarify and to illuminate existing teaching which had fired Luther and Calvin. The intellectual fearlessness of all these individuals was a fearlessness which allowed them to consider new ideas and ways of looking at the world: by the end of the seventeenth century the new 'rational' religion of

Protestantism had ended much superstition and allowed people to explore radically new possibilities about the relationship between human beings and the natural world. But neither the end of the sixteenth century nor the end of the seventeenth saw final breaks between one world and the other, cultures did not change completely in the course of a hundred years and, as historical accounts of England in the sixteenth century have shown, old and new religions, old and new ideas remained part and parcel of the social world. But the idea of human beings being able to understand the world, independent of the teaching of the Catholic Church, had taken hold with a vitality and a determination which signal the beginning of the modern.

Chapter 2

Reason, Revolution and Reaction

1618–48 The Thirty Years War
1637 Publication of *Discourse on Method* by Descartes
1649 Execution of Charles I of England
1656 Completion of *Las Meninas* by Velasquez
1687 Publication of Isaac Newton's *Principia Mathematica*
1702 Founding of St Petersburg by Peter the Great
1772 Lord Mansfield delivers the judgement that slavery is illegal in British dominions
1776 Declaration of Independence of the United States of America
1776 Publication of *The Wealth of Nations* by Adam Smith
1789 The attack on the Bastille; beginning of the French Revolution
1790 Publication of *Reflections on the Revolution in France* by Edmund Burke
1792 Publication of *A Vindication of the Rights of Woman* by Mary Wollstonecraft
1818 Publication of *Frankenstein* by Mary Shelley

'Oh my America! My new-found-land' wrote the poet and cleric John Donne at the end of the sixteenth century. Donne (1572–1631) is writing in praise of the erotic, but that particular line in his poem is often taken as indicative of the spirit of the late sixteenth and early seventeenth centuries, a spirit of exploration and change, ageless curiosity about the world now realized in the 'discovery' of new worlds and new peoples. The world of the early seventeenth century was known to be round; not only were there new worlds outside the old worlds (something which had always been suspected and part of mythology) but these new worlds were rapidly becoming part of the social and political reality of the states of Europe. Mariners of Spain, England and Portugal had all made journeys to the Americas by the middle of the sixteenth century; Spain had claimed extensive lands in Central and South America and England had founded colonies on the eastern shore of what was to become the United States. This was not the first time that countries had claimed overseas or foreign territory (England itself had been a Roman colony for almost five hundred years), but new forms of technology and new attitudes to the social world started to change the relationship between the colony and the colonizing state. These changes were by no means immediately apparent: for example, the behaviour of the Spanish in Latin America in the sixteenth century was that of straightforward plunder and subjugation. Treasure ships from the Americas sailed up the Guadalquivir river to Seville and were used to finance the building of churches and Spanish wars in other parts of Europe. Yet by the end of the period with which this chapter is concerned (the end of the eighteenth century), the people of a colony – namely the people of the United States – had rethought their relationship to their governing power and given the world the blueprint for a new form of constitutional and democratic government.

However, between the end of the sixteenth century and 1776 (the year of the Declaration of Independence in Philadelphia) there lay almost two hundred years in which European thought underwent a transformation as radical as that of the Reformation and the Renaissance. That transformation is generally known as the Enlightenment and its approximate boundaries are represented by – at its emergence – the work of René Descartes (1596–1650) born in France but spending much of his adult life in Holland, and, at its conclusion, the work of Immanuel Kant (1724–1804) living and working in Germany in the second half of the eighteenth century. By the time Kant was writing, intellectual life had started to assume those distinctions between subjects and disciplines which we can recognize in the twenty-first century. In contrast, at the time that Descartes was writing, these distinctions had not yet emerged and many notable figures of the seventeenth century would have had difficulty in identifying themselves with a particular intellectual specialization. Descartes himself first studied mathematics and then, in 1637 published *Discourse on Method*, a book which is generally taken to be the first text in modern philosophy. What Descartes did in this work was, in the view of many philosophers, to establish that the modern theory of knowledge must address the two questions, 'How do I know?' and 'Can I be certain?'

The importance of Descartes' work was not that he used it to disprove the existence of God, or to turn his back on the idea of religious belief, but that he made belief subject to reason. He did not argue that we can prove, in a final or conclusive manner, the existence of God, but he did suggest that we can examine the process through which we come to claim that God exists. It was this way of thinking that came to hold a central place in the history of the Enlightenment. But, and it is a very important but, God remains the definitive and transcendent power in the universe. That centrality of God was evident in the work of Descartes' contemporary, the French writer Blaise Pascal (1623–62) whose *Pensées* asserted the rational capacity of human beings, within a world still governed by God.

In establishing the work of Descartes (one of the three great Rationalists of the Enlightenment, the others being Benedict de Spinoza (1632–77), and Gottfried Leibniz (1646–1716)) as the beginning of the European Enlightenment, what may puzzle some readers of the secular twenty-first century is that God, and belief in God, are still very much part of the philosophical world. God does not 'die', in the sense of becoming an optional part of philosophy, until the nineteenth century, and until that time the existence of a world without God was alien to the great majority of those who were concerned with philosophical and political questions. But what was changing recognizably amongst those who were concerned with these issues was the basis of belief: belief in God was no longer to be achieved through obedience to the teachings of a church but through thought and a rational process of understanding. This is to make a conventional claim for the Enlightenment: the claim that assumes that what was characteristic of this movement was a movement towards rational thought. Yet this assumption disallows important and scholarly debates of previous centuries in which ideas about God, Creation and the Universe were part of intellectual life. This point is made in order to suggest that what occurred in the seventeenth and eighteenth centuries was not the sudden emergence of intellectual curiosity in Europe but the shifting of the relationship between power (particularly political and ecclesiastical power) and knowledge. An important part of this shift was the opening up of a secular space for the discussion of social organization (such as was evident in the work of Thomas Hobbes (1588–1679) and the investigation of the natural world.

The Europe of the seventeenth century, in which these debates took place, was, for many of its citizens, a place of danger and disruption. Germany, France and England all endured various forms of civil strife, plague remained a consistent danger (London was decimated by plague by 1666) and the various forms of Christian churches still fought both against each other and against those of their subjects whom they regarded as either disobedient or sub-versive. The most notable 'show trial' between knowledge and enquiry and ecclesiastical authority was that of Galileo (1564–1642) in 1634, when he was summoned before the Inquisition to account for his view that the sun was the centre of the universe. What Galileo had done was to design a refracting telescope with which he was able to confirm the earlier observation of Copernicus (1473–1543) that the sun is the centre of the system of the heavens. Galileo also suggested that the Milky Way was part of a huge galaxy of stars. These deductions, made by Galileo without any wish to threaten or undermine the Catholic Church, were nevertheless taken as deeply dangerous ideas and it was only through outside intervention that Galileo was saved from punishment by the Italian Inquisition.

In the twenty-first century, what may seem curious about these debates between Galileo and the papacy is that what Galileo essen-tially wanted to do – besides outline a theory of the planets – was to make navigation safer. It might be supposed today that prosaic self-interest would have encouraged the papacy (or indeed anyone else who was likely to get on board a ship) to work as hard as possible to ensure accurate navigational devices. Given that putting out to sea in the sixteenth and seventeenth centuries was always a hazardous business, it is difficult for us to understand why anyone would have wished to crush a form of enquiry likely to save one's own, as much as anyone else's, life. But to suppose this would overlook two possi-bilities of the relationship between power and knowledge which remain important. The first is that all societies – and those of the twentieth and twenty-first centuries are no exception to this – do not always regard the pursuit of knowledge with an unreserved welcome. The second is that many societies regard the upholding of authority *per se* as far more important than the claims of evident intellectual advance. The examples of absurd science in Stalin's Russia (the adoption of the genetic theories of Lysenko in 1948 being the best-known instance) and the contemporary battles in the United States between creationism and theories of evolution all suggest that the idea of the absolute triumph of the ideals of the Enlightenment is somewhat premature.

The seventeenth century thus contains, as do most other cen-turies, examples of hugely innovative ideas and equally considerable forms of resistance. At the same time it is also important to recognize that advances in human knowledge do not occur only out of human curiosity or the wish to advance knowledge but are also directed towards the solution of problems in human existence and everyday reality. The example of Galileo serves to illustrate precisely that relationship between scientific enquiry and the needs of the social world which is suggested above: Galileo wanted to solve the problem of longitude, and was willing to attempt to collect the life pension offered by Philip III of Spain to the person who produced a solution. Philip III had announced this prize in 1598 and although Galileo was never to collect the prize it offers a wonderful example of the complexities of the relationships between social pressures, religion and the pursuit of knowledge. Here was an explicitly Catholic monarch offering a prize for scientific advance, a prize in large part motivated by the wish to ensure the safe passage to Spain of the laden treasure ships from the Americas. But as we have seen, the papacy, the spiritual authority to which Philip III subjected himself, had no wish to see its version of the universe overthrown and could not countenance an alternative view of the world.

The particular case of Galileo has been taken by many writers on the seventeenth century, and both the history of the Enlightenment and the history of science, to suggest that the rise of Protestantism in the sixteenth century divided Europe not just in religious terms but also in terms of attitudes to intellectual enquiry. One of the best known of these accounts is that of Robert Merton, who follows Max Weber in arguing that there was an affinity between Protestantism and scientific enquiry which was distinct from that of Catholicism.[1] Both Merton and Weber observed that the progress of science in the seventeenth century (and in particular its institutional recognition and support by central governments) was considerably stronger and more noticeable in Protestant parts of Europe or in countries where rulers adopted relatively laissez-faire attitudes towards religion. Yet it could also be suggested that this division of Europe – essentially between the scientific/rational north and the non-scientific/Catholic south – ignores those advances in the representation of the human condition which lie outside scientific enquiry and are more generally considered as a part of literary or visual art. Spain gave Europe the first novel (Cervantes published *Don Quixote* in 1605) and perhaps the first most self-conscious painting, in Velazquez's *Las Meninas* (painted in 1656 and used on the cover of this book). Since we regard narrative fiction and self-consciousness as two of the essential elements of 'the modern', it is perhaps over-hasty to accept divisions between parts of Europe which seem to suggest advance in one and reaction in others. It is equally important to recognize that when Merton and Weber wrote about science and religion they did not suggest that Protestantism gave rise to science in any direct or causal way but rather that between Protestantism and science there lay an affinity which was characterized by a willingness to experiment and examine. This affinity was then sharpened and developed by the specific demands of a particular situation, but it is not an argument that equates Protestantism with the emergence of human curiosity or a wish to examine the natural world. Merton writes thus: 'But it is not sufficient verification of our hypothesis to indicate the favourable social attitudes to science induced by the Protestant ethic ... nor that the cast of thought which is characteristic of modern science, namely, the combination of empiricism and rationalism and the faith in the validity of one basic postulate, an apprehensible order in Nature, bears an other than fortuitous congruence with the attitudes involved in Protestantism.'[2]

One further point which we need to emphasize about the work of both Merton and Weber on science is that both are working with the expectation that the people and the societies that they are writing about have an individual belief in God. Yet it is in the seventeenth century that we can start to trace the emergence of the modern view that belief in God (be it a Catholic or a Jewish or a Protestant God) is optional. Galileo and Descartes both worked within the boundaries of a world view organized by belief in God; other formidable writers (such as Hobbes), and groups of people (such as the English Quakers) in the seventeenth century were less sure about this and started to nail their colours to the mast of scepticism about religion, if not actual atheism.

What we can see in the seventeenth century are three emergent traditions about religion and knowledge. The first is that of 'old' Europe, an absolute acceptance of everything taught by the Catholic priest and a set of beliefs which probably include a good deal of superstition and sorcery. The second is a tradition of what might be described as 'secular' or enlightened belief, that is a continued acceptance of the idea of God, and worship through a particular church, but beliefs which reject superstition and assert the right of the individual to engage with the questioning and examination of religion. The third, and most radical and innovative, tradition is that of the outright rejection of the idea of God. The person who did more than any other to further this tradition was the Dutch philosopher

Spinoza, a man whose career brings together many of the complexities of seventeenth-century Europe.

Benedict de Spinoza was a native of Amsterdam, a city in a country which had fought a long and bitter war for its independence from Spain and the authority of Spanish Catholicism. Spinoza came from a Portuguese Jewish background and because of his Jewish identity had been barred from a conventional university education. However, he very effectively taught himself the essentials of existing philosophy (including a familiarization with the work of Descartes), and such was his success in this endeavour that his two major philosophical works (*Tractatus Theologico-Politicus* of 1670 and *Ethics* of 1670) became seen as the founding works of disbelief (or absence of belief) in God. These works proved to be too radical for the Dutch state: despite the traditions of a country which had had to fight for its own religious freedom, the work of Spinoza was simply too challenging for the Dutch authorities and it was banned.

But what did not happen to Spinoza was burning at the stake or a trial before the Inquisition. Nor did Spinoza see his work vanish from Europe, and both his major works were widely circulated in French and can be traced as part of the general intellectual heritage of the time. Spinoza, like his contemporary Hobbes, raised for European culture the possibility that God did not exist. Hobbes was to go further than Spinoza is his public scepticism about the existence of God and belief in the Christian Trinity, but both men represent the emerging willingness of individuals to question what, for many people, had been (and still was) the bedrock of European civilization, namely a belief in a Christian God. If one of the ironies of Spinoza's career is that the apparently free-thinking Dutch found his work too much to tolerate, then another is the fact that the Jewish Spinoza played a crucial part in bringing into being that Enlightenment which, to some critics, was notable for its part in the genesis of the Holocaust.

The work of Spinoza was part of those religious wars, written and military, which were fought throughout Europe in the seventeenth century. Compared with the sixteenth century, which had seen the emergence of Protestant Christianity, the seventeenth was far more violent in the fury with which individuals pursued both their own religious beliefs and those of others. In England, religion played a considerable part in the origins of the Civil Wars of 1642–51, many non-conformists (in particular, Puritans) found it necessary to leave the country to find religious freedom, and throughout the century

Parliament went on passing Acts of various kinds both to exclude Roman Catholics from civil society and to produce religious conformity amongst Protestants. (For example, in 1697–98 Parliament passed an Act for the suppression of blasphemy, which was an attempt to maintain belief in the Trinity.) By the end of the seventeenth century, Protestantism had been secured as the dominant religion of England, with Catholics barred from succession to the throne. On the other side of the Channel in France, Catholicism had been re-established as the dominant religion when, in 1685, Louis XIV revoked the Edict of Nantes and rekindled antagonism towards the Huguenots. In Germany and other parts of northern and central Europe the Thirty Years War of 1618–48 led to considerable loss of life and social chaos; only in Spain and Italy was Catholicism so little challenged as to rule out the possibility of bitter social strife. Thus set against the emergence of Enlightenment scepticism and nascent secularism, what we can see is the persistence of views about religion which were sufficiently passionately held to produce civil wars and persecution. As in most centuries from 1500 to 1900, religious strife largely took the form of contests and conflicts between various forms of Christianity. Yet it is important not to forget that another conflict was also a consistent part of the European experience: the persecution of the Jews. European anti-Semitism has a long history and what can be observed over the course of about five hundred years is that the persecution and intolerance did not disappear, rather that the context of anti-Semitism changed over time. If England was notably and viciously anti-Semitic in the twelfth century, then the same was true of Spain in the fifteenth. What emerged from these different experiences was the establishment of centres of Jewish culture (Prague in the seventeenth century being a notable example) and different degrees of toleration and assimilation in different European societies.

The wars and strife produced by religious intolerance in Europe in the seventeenth century led, of course, to terrible personal hardships and losses. For many people, staying in the same place became too dangerous or too difficult and thus it is that in the seventeenth century we see the emergence of very marked patterns of migration and relocation. The most dramatic example of this was the arrival of the *Mayflower* and the Pilgrim Fathers in Massachusetts in 1620. This motley band of people, some motivated by the desire for religious freedom and others by more complex motives, set up a colony that was to emerge as the first nation to commit itself explicitly to the separation of state and nation and religion. This profoundly modern idea was not to come to fruition until 1776 and the writing of the Declaration of Independence (a document in which God still appears as a central character) and for many years the settlements of Massachusetts were as intolerant as any that had been left behind in Europe. But they were typical of the forced migration of peoples for religious reasons: for example, of French Huguenots to England and of German Protestants and Catholics alike to those parts of Germany more accepting of a particular version of Christianity. Yet whilst we speak of divisions between particular forms of Christianity it is also important to remember that Christianity (and indeed other religions) contained much that was part of a particular culture quite as much as being specifically theological.

The quotation from John Donne with which this chapter opened is one of the most quoted love poems of English literature. It was written in Donne's youth, before he took Holy Orders at the age of 43 and subsequently became Dean of St Paul's in London. The poem, like the sonnets of Shakespeare or passages from his plays, expresses joy and delight in the sensuous, a celebration of the possibilities of the body, which is very far from what we might expect of a Protestant culture at the beginning of the seventeenth century. In the poem what we see are the complex elements of a culture which cannot be understood only in terms of sharp divisions between Protestant and Catholic. A part of English history which has often been taken as a given is the idea that the Reformation made the English into Protestants and destroyed older ideas and expectations. But what Donne's poem should remind us is that cultures are often resistant to social and political change and that although we can locate Puritan values in the culture of the seventeenth century, so too can we locate the kind of vibrant humanism which Donne's poem exemplifies. Nor, in seventeenth century Europe, was Donne alone in his enjoyment of the physical and the creative world. German Baroque of the seventeenth-century, the growing fascination in northern Europe with Palladio and the architecture of Italy, and the continuing literary energy of the theatre, all speak of the heritage of the Renaissance and the growing self-confidence of vernacular and popular cultures.

Perhaps the most famous building of seventeenth-century Europe is the palace built by Louis XIV at Versailles in France. Palaces were hardly unknown in Europe by this time but the magnificence and splendour of Versailles was a new standard in the achievements of European architecture. Part of what Versailles was about was the veneration – in bricks and mortar – of secular power. But an important part of that power lay not simply in the jurisdiction of the king over his subjects (and certainly Louis XIV embodied, far more than other European monarchs of the seventeenth century, the idea of absolute power), but also in the cultural and intellectual authority of the monarch. Louis XIV – and Charles II of England – took the view that the monarch should promote and support the arts and the sciences. Again, patronage was no new idea in European history, but what these monarchs did was to bring together intellectual life and the interests of the state. To this end, Louis XIV founded the Académie Française, Charles II the Royal Society: both exercises in the self-conscious recognition that ideas mattered in a society and that being at the forefront of ideas was part of the identity of a powerful nation. It was an exercise to be copied by Peter the Great in 1702 in the founding of what was to become St Petersburg in Russia, and continued in the same country by the energy with which Catherine the Great pursued great works of art and the company of famous intellectuals, most notably the Frenchman, François-Marie Arouet, more generally known as Voltaire (1694–1778). These monarchies were thus not simply about the exercise of power but also about the making of a national identity through support of, and association with, the arts and the social sciences. For the absolute monarchs of France and Russia the idea was to end unhappily, since ideas, once encouraged and supported, proved to be impossible to control. But this support, widespread across Europe from the seventeenth century onwards and demonstrated by the fact that many of the great names of European culture can be shown to have had support from one monarch or another, provided, crucially, another social location for ideas other than in churches.

The world of ideas, had, therefore, moved, by the end of the seventeenth century to more diverse locations than that of religious orders and the church. The material world of the seventeenth, and indeed much of the eighteenth century, had taken no similarly great leap forward. The eminent English historian J.H. Plumb wrote of England at the beginning of the eighteenth century in profound horror at the conditions of squalor, want and disease in which the majority of the population lived. Thus he observed that, whilst the majority of the population lived and worked on the land, there were some towns. However, he wrote, 'The first noticeable thing about these towns would have been the stench. ... The houses of the poor were one or two room hovels. ... Disease was rampant and unchecked: smallpox, typhus, typhoid and dysentery made death a commonplace. ... In the early part of the century, only about one child in four, born in London, survived and probably the infant mortality was higher in the mushroom towns of the north.'[3] Plumb is writing specifically of England, but these conditions would have been replicated in other European countries and in some of those countries, less rich than England, the conditions in which the majority of the population lived were worse than those which Plumb describes.

Europe at the end of the seventeenth century was not, historical evidence suggests, a continent in which the population as a whole had begun to enjoy or know many of the advances of science or political philosophy made in those years. In the main, the terrible religious wars of the century had come to an end and civil peace had arrived. But the century which had opened with the post-Renaissance flowering of the arts still evident, and the first works of the Enlightenment about to be written, had not seen an accompanying improvement in the material lot of the majority of European populations. This, in the eighteenth century, was about to change, as were the direction and the force of intellectual innovation. In England in particular, two aspects of late-seventeenth-century and early-eighteenth-century history were to secure this advance. The first was the political settlement of 1688 which brought William of Orange and his wife Mary to the throne of England and established the space for a degree of representational democracy. The second was the continued development of practical science: the late seventeenth century had seen the work of William Harvey (1578–1657) on the circulation of blood and of Isaac Newton (1643–1727) on physics. But the first years of the eighteenth century were to see innovations which had a more dramatic impact on the production of material goods, innovations which were to begin to displace the ancient relationship between the production of goods and human labour: industrial technology was beginning to arrive. Thus in the first two decades of the eighteenth century England saw the introduction of the steam engine of Newcomen in 1712 (an improvement on Savery's 1698 steam pump, it made deep-seam mining possible), the use of coke for smelting (in 1713) and the building of a factory to make silk yarn (in 1716).

These innovations – and others like them were to continue throughout Europe in the eighteenth century – were designed, primarily, to make possible the greater production of goods and to make richer and more prosperous those people who made their living out of trade. If, by the end of the eighteenth century, some of the English population lived a more comfortable and less hazardous life than that of their ancestors at the beginning of the century it was largely because many of their number had been drawn into the growing infrastructure which supported trade and industry. Indeed, the safeguarding of these activities became an organizing principle of governments throughout Europe, all of which recognized the centrality of material wealth to political power. Peter the Great, for example, wanted to construct a city on the banks of the River Neva not just because of a fascination with all things European, and with Italian architecture in particular, but also because he identified the importance of a relatively ice-free port for his country's trading interests. In this calculation – and others made by other European monarchs – what can be seen is a shift towards 'merchant capitalism', the form of economic relations which views trade not simply as a way of securing certain goods but as a way of making money and securing markets for manufactured goods. The centrality of capital for economic growth had been recognized, by the beginning of the eighteenth century, by many Europeans.

But one form of capital which was to produce terrible consequences for millions of people was that of human capital, and specifically slavery. Itself an ancient form of human relationship it had become a major, if always contested, fact of European life by the middle of the eighteenth century and the infamous 'slave triangle' between England, West Africa and the Caribbean had brought horror to the lives of transported Africans. Although most transported Africans were taken to work on the plantations of the Caribbean, a small number were also brought to England; by the second half of the eighteenth century it is estimated that there were about ten thousand slaves in England, mostly working in agriculture or as servants. In 1772, Lord Mansfield made the celebrated judgement that slavery was illegal in England, but the full abolition of slavery in the British Empire was not to take place until 1833.

What the slave trade brought together were two crucial eighteenth-century concerns. One was the question of trade, and the proper way to conduct trade, with fierce arguments both for and against the idea of free trade. Adam Smith was to put the case for free trade most forcefully in his *Enquiry into the Wealth of Nations* (1776), but the question was to continue to be a matter of intense political debate until the latter part of the nineteenth century. The second issue of which slavery is a part is that of the crucial eighteenth-century concern with the nature of the relationship between a state and its people. It was this concern, more than any other, which gave rise to two of the best-known of the dates in the eighteenth century: the Declaration of Independence in what was to become the United States of America in1776, and the French Revolution of 1789. Both of these dramatic shifts in the reordering of the political life of the west (with consequences that were to last, in both cases, for decades afterwards) arose in part out of debates and ideas of the Enlightenment, but they also emerged out of specific social transformations and political circumstances.

Earlier in this chapter the works of writers of the seventeenth-century Enlightenment – Descartes, Hobbes, Spinoza – were identified as part of a shift towards the rethinking of the relationship between religion and the social world. None of these individuals specifically advocated a secular society as we would understand it in the twenty-first century (although perhaps Hobbes comes close), but what they all did was to ask questions about the authority of traditional judgements about the existence of God. This did not, in itself, lead to a loss of belief or the coming of a secular world, but it did open up a social and intellectual space for the examination of both the natural and the social world. Science in the seventeenth century was the first discipline to take up this possibility: as we have seen, Galileo, Newton, Harvey and others all made use of this space and in doing so implicitly made it clear that they did not regard the account of the Bible as the definitive account of the making of the physical world or as sufficiently informed to provide an explanation for all natural phenomena. What is important here again is the idea of unintended consequences: individuals working in particular contexts were concerned with particular problems (some of them arising from ordinary human experience), none had a self-conscious sense of taking part in what is now termed 'the Enlightenment' or, with an even more focused sense of intention, 'the Enlightenment Project'.

By the beginning of the eighteenth century the progress of science and nascent industrial technology, together with dramatic political events such as the execution of Charles I of England in 1649, had begun to foster a sense that not only could the world be understood (which is an idea as old as European civilization) but it could also be controlled. The English had shown that the political world could be rethought and remade, access to the Bible had made accessible the central text of European culture, and science was beginning to establish the idea that the natural world – and, for example, travel within it – could be made predictable. It is impossible to name one person who represents, from the end of the seventeenth century onwards, 'the Enlightenment' (or even less so the much more intentional 'Enlightenment Project'), but amongst the names that are always regarded as crucial in the one hundred years before the French Revolution are Hobbes, Locke and Hume in England, Voltaire, Diderot and Rousseau (1712–78) in France, and Kant in Germany. Of these people it is perhaps Denis Diderot (1713–84) who was the most influential in his lifetime; his seventeen-volume *Encyclopaedia* (composed with help from Voltaire) brought together the eighteenth-century passion for the collection of knowledge and a radical commitment to free speech and critical discussion. But all these writers (known to each other, but not always in agreement as, for example, in the case of Rousseau and Voltaire) shared the view that the starting point for knowledge was open and free enquiry into human understanding.

One aspect of the list above which may occur to many readers is its masculinity: no women appear as figures in any list of Enlightenment luminaries and it is not until the end of the eighteenth century that we can name women who become central figures in various creative and intellectual traditions – Mary Wollstonecraft (1759–97) in political science for example, and Jane Austen (1775–1817) in the history of the novel. But this absence of women should not lead us to accept the view that it was not until the 'emancipation' of women in the nineteenth century that women began to take a more public place in intellectual life. Women, as numerous scholars have now shown, were crucial in establishing many of the networks of intellectual life and in participation in the worlds of art and letters. But as important to future debates about gender and knowledge was what Thomas Laqueur has described as the 'invention' of sex.[4] By this Laqueur does not mean that the eighteenth century was the first to recognize sexual difference. What he does mean is that in the west in the eighteenth century men and women became seen, for the first time, as two distinct genders, women being distinctly 'female' rather than a different version of male. Again, what we can trace here is a dimuition of the authority of the Bible as an account of the social and physical world: as long as the story of the Creation named women as 'Adam's Rib' then they would inevitably be seen in terms which identified the human as male. It has taken centuries (and is arguably still continuing) for the understanding of 'human' or 'people' to be enlarged beyond that of masculinity, but it was in the eighteenth century that we can see the beginning of that sense of gender difference which was to become a part of the history of nineteenth- and twentieth-century Europe. By the end of the eighteenth century we can see that the category of 'woman' has been recognized within European culture and within economic markets: literature, commodities, social guidance and political campaigns all begin to exist specifically for women.

Whilst it is possible to see the emergence of gender difference as a significant social factor throughout the eighteenth century, one area in which gender played a relatively limited but not insignificant part was in those social events for which the eighteenth century is best known. The Revolution in the United States was made by men, the Constitution of the United States, written by what has been described as the greatest committee in history (it included Benjamin Franklin and Thomas Jefferson), began with the words: 'all men are created equal'. In the same way, the rallying cry of revolutionaries in France was 'Liberty, Equality and Fraternity'. Even if we recognize that the words 'men' and 'fraternity' (brotherhood) were used in the eighteenth century without any sense of that problematic relationship to gender which we have acquired in the twenty-first century, it is still the case that the political ideals embraced in both France and the United States did not recognize the question of gender.

But in another sense, if we leave aside the failure to recognize the claims of women as much as men to a space in civil society, the rallying cries of revolutionaries in both France and the United States show the truly dramatic distance which had been travelled between the beginning of the seventeenth and the end of the eighteenth centuries. At the beginning of the seventeenth century, James I of England could assert, and be taken quite seriously when doing so, that he had a divine right to rule and that the hand of God would strike down those who opposed his authority. By the end of the eighteenth century this kind of belief had been marginalized in much of Europe: autocracy certainly remained (and the association between God and ruler was to remain in Russia throughout the nineteenth century), but in most of Europe there was a recognition that rulers were such by accident of birth and that the social organization of government and authority was a matter for negotiation within the social world. Even the unfortunate Louis XVI of France, guillotined by the revolutionary French government, had come to recognize that a monarch had to accept constraints on his power. For various reasons Louis was unable to move quickly, or radically, enough to satisfy emergent political demands, but it is clear that even in the case of this monarch, who is emblematic of the fall of European absolutism, there was a befuddled awareness that the 'old regime' could not continue for ever.

The French Revolution and the American Declaration of Independence are both pivotal moments in the history of the west, moments on which it is not an exaggeration to say that the world changed. In the case of France, aspects of social life which had been taken for granted for generations (for example the authority of the clergy and that of the aristocracy) disappeared within the space of ten years and were replaced by new forms of social regulation such as secular, state marriage ceremonies and a reordering of patterns of land owning in some parts of France. In the same way, in the nascent United States, people who had previously supposed themselves to be citizens of the British Crown now discovered that they were, after all, citizens of an entirely new country, which was in the equally novel process of making up its own rules and writing its own constitution, a constitution which was to suggest to its readers not only the duties of the citizen towards the state but also the expectations which the citizen might reasonably have of the state (most extraordinarily the pursuit of happiness). These two cultures – of France and of the United States – were to come together in the work of one of the first, and most perceptive, writers about the United States, the Frenchman Alexis de Tocqueville (1805–59). Writing between 1835 and 1840 in his *Democracy in America*, de Tocqueville remarked, 'I find no parallel for what is occurring before my eyes'. De Tocqueville was to go on to express amazement at the degree of social democracy in the United States, an absence of the sense of the social hierarchy, which in his view had never disappeared from Europe.

It would appear from the work of de Tocqueville (and other travellers across the Atlantic in the early nineteenth century) that the new society being formed in the United States was a genuinely different one from that of Europe. This perception of the United States has led various writers to suggest that the United States was the true political result of the Enlightenment, since the French Revolution, and the French revolutionary government, had been quite rapidly replaced by the more socially conservative policies of Napoleon Bonaparte (1769–1821) and his successors. Bonaparte threw many sections of European society (not least in Britain) into panic and concern; indeed, his military campaigns were an obvious threat to British trading interests. Nevertheless, his domestic policies did not continue the more radical aspects of the politics of the period immediately after 1789, and his years in power in France were not characterized by any determination to overthrow social hierarchies, least of all the idea that one person – notably himself – might have supreme social power. But what Napoleon did do was to effect considerable changes in the organization of the French state: the law was codified (the *Code Civil*, for example, still forms the basis of French civil law) and education, science and the arts encouraged.

For the British, Napoleon (and the much reorganized French state and its army) became a genuine figure of fear at the end of the eighteenth and beginning of the nineteenth century, and a generation of men, on either a voluntary or a forced basis, were much concerned with military exercises against him. But what we need to consider, in looking back at the seventeenth and the eighteenth centuries, is the extent to which the great political events for which these centuries are known (the execution of Charles I, the Glorious Revolution in 1688, the Declaration of Independence and the French Revolution), together with the great works produced in the course of the Enlightenment, actually impinged on the lives of the majority of the citizens of Europe of those centuries. In one sense, that of the language in which 'ordinary' people are described, both the intellectual and the political events made a significant difference, in that 'people' or 'subjects' became 'citizens', a way of describing a population which underlines both the relationship between person and the state or nation and the essentially egalitarian nature of the relationship between human individuals. Becoming a 'citizen', which for many, although not all, was part of European life by the end of the eighteenth century, was the most obvious way in which the ideas of the Enlightenment found their expression in a new political language. That language was then closely related to the expectations that came with it: in particular the expectation that citizens would share in the making of political decisions. The existence of a popular 'voice' was no new thing in European history (even though it was consistently conceptualized by those in authority as 'the mob'), but from the sixteenth century onwards, and very much so in the eighteenth century, what can be seen to be emerging as a political force and a political presence was the 'voice of the people'. The view of large groups of ordinary people expressing their political views could still be seen as 'the rabble', but it had become evident by the end of the eighteenth century that the rabble could play an important part in the course of events.

But a new political language did not emerge, for most people, out of a study of the works of John Locke, Voltaire or Kant. Rates of literacy throughout Europe in the seventeenth and eighteenth centuries were not high and the reality of almost universal literacy was not to emerge until late in the nineteenth century. Assessments of literacy vary between European societies, with northern Europe having generally higher rates than southern, but it was not to improve dramatically anywhere until the beginning of the nineteenth century. Few people had any real or consistent schooling and many of the great social movements which affected large numbers of people, for example the rise of Methodism in Britain, were the result of verbal, rather than print, cultures. But one aspect of print culture did change in the eighteenth century, which was less about how many people read than about what people read. The change was that, particularly in Britain, people began to write, publish and read newspapers and periodicals and write, and read, novels. The reason for these new forms of print cultures was in part the expansion of trade and the development of urban culture and urban life. The relative peace of the eighteenth century, together with better and more reliable methods of navigation, made trade both more extensive and more complex. With this grew the demand for information, for contracts, for a way of communicating with others the processes and the demands of these new enterprises. Traders needed to know about new places, merchants and traders needed to know about government policies, and many people living in cities both needed and wanted to know about events outside their immediate world. For this new world, traditional forms of literature – the epic poems of John Milton or Alexander Pope – were singularly inappropriate. The theatre still flourished, in both Britain and France, but in Britain in particular there developed in the eighteenth century a form of literature which was to give voice to new perceptions about the world.

As we have seen, the British cannot claim to have written the first novel. That place in literary history belongs to Cervantes and to his novel *Don Quixote*. But for all kinds of reasons the development of the novel in Spain did not flower in the same way as in England in the eighteenth century, when the novel began to articulate a definably new tradition in social life, the articulation and discussion of the problems facing ordinary people in their lives. The 'ordinary' people who constituted the characters of the great English novels of the eighteenth century, for example those of Daniel Defoe (1660–1731), Samuel Richardson (1689–1761), Henry Fielding (1707–54) and Tobias Smollett (1721–71), had a huge social range, and included characters from all walks and conditions of society. This in itself was no different from the range of characters in Shakespeare, but what the novel did was to examine individual human motivation and to allow readers to share in the choices faced by the central characters. All English novels of the eighteenth century also had much to say about gender relations: whilst authors of the eighteenth century may not have recognized that they lived in a century which had invented gender difference, what they all recognized were the frequent diffi- culties of relations between the sexes and the many unresolved questions which existed for everyone in the so-called private sphere of the household. It is this discussion of the 'private' lives of indi- viduals which makes the novel such an important part of the history of western social life.

The extension of print culture which occurred in England in the eighteenth century and which the anthropologist Ernest Gellner has argued was instrumental in forming the idea of a 'national culture' brought with it changes in the idea of what constituted the public and the private spheres.[5] On this question, by far the most important thesis is that of the German sociologist Jurgen Habermas, who has outlined what he sees as an emerging division in the eighteenth century between the literary and the political.[6] For Habermas, the public or political sphere is any place where two or more people come together – with an entirely self-conscious understanding – that they are talking politics. The private sphere, on the other hand, is that of individual contemplation, the place that the modern world associates in term of physical space with the private, or, in terms of conceptual space, the context (and it is here that literature is so important) where the interior self is examined and discussed. Using this idea it is possible to show how Habermas's distinction between the literary and the political offers us a very useful way of seeing the developments that took place in the eighteenth and early nineteenth centuries in the discussion of the affairs of both the person and the world. It is conventionally agreed that the eighteenth century saw the emergence of numerous 'political' spaces (the coffee house and salon being two frequently quoted examples, whilst a greater social inclusiveness would also add the Nonconformist chapel and the public house), but these places are only part of what Habermas means by the 'political' space. For Habermas the space is not so much about bricks and mortar as about spoken exchanges which are, as he describes it, a 'performative utterance'. That is to say, the people speaking have realized that what they are saying is not 'private' but is political, in the sense that their words have meaning and, most importantly, carry meaning and consequences. When the London Stock Exchange took as its motto 'My Word is my Bond', those who coined the phrase recognized that people speaking together could make binding contracts. Thus what Habermas offers us is a way of understanding the changes that took place in the eighteenth century aside from those evident developments in, for example, the growth of the reading public.

As already suggested, one issue which is central to almost all eighteenth-century English novels is the question of how to order relations between men and women. In past decades, historians, notably Phillipe Aries and Lawrence Stone, have suggested that from the seventeenth century onwards Europe saw the emergence of 'modern' attitudes towards children and the growth of the aspiration of an affectionate, rather than socially functional, marriage.[7] Although this idea is now regarded with some scepticism, the evidence of print culture in the eighteenth century suggests that novelists (and their readers) were very much interested in the question of how to have and how to ensure a 'happy' marriage. The fullest discussion of this idea by a male novelist is in Samuel Richardson's lengthy novel *Clarissa*; the fullest discussion by a woman writer is the work of Jane Austen (1775–1817). Their works differ vastly in composition and narrative form, but what both agree on is the right of women to be thought of as equal, rational partners in a marriage and for the rights of women to choose marriage partners to be taken seriously. The 'emancipation' of women is often interpreted in terms of women's access to education and employment, but there is a strong case to be made for the real emancipation of women lying in the eighteenth-century articulation of the rights of women in the 'private' sphere. Feminist critics of patriarchal law have made much of the absence of the rights of women in law before the twentieth century, and although the impact of this formidable patriarchal bias can be exaggerated in terms of its impact on individuals it was certainly the case that what eighteenth-century fiction was doing was to initiate opposition to the idea that the rule of men over women was justifiable. Samuel Richardson, for example, exposed the gendered bias of social rules about sexual morality, Henry Fielding defended the right of women to choose their own husbands, and Jane Austen advanced the view that marriage should only be entered by people who had some basis for the possibility of a rational relationship. What we can see in these approaches to the establishment or renegotiation of marriage is both the voice of the Enlightenment and stress on the value of thought, rational appreciation of other individuals and a greater sense of social democracy.

In Jane Austen's novel *Mansfield Park*, Sir Thomas Bertram, the patriarch of the estate of Mansfield, reproaches Fanny Price, the penniless heroine, for refusing an advantageous marriage. In his tirade against Fanny, Sir Thomas accuses Fanny of that 'independence of spirit, which prevails so much in modern days, even in young women'. The accusation is a definitive summary of all those fears about the changing social and political world that were voiced in Europe at the end of the eighteenth century. The French Revolution of 1789 and the Declaration of the Rights of Man in the same year had been hailed by radicals across the Continent as the beginning of a new age of freedom and liberty, but the savagery of the Terror in France and the execution of Louis XVI and Marie Antoinette in 1793 had made the Revolution look rather less than attractive to those with conservative inclinations. In England the writer Edmund Burke (1729–97), himself once a proponent of the Dunning Resolution of 1780 that 'the power of the Crown has increased, is increasing, and ought to be diminished', was appalled by the Revolution in France and expressed these views in 1790 in *Reflections on the Revolution in France*. (Burke had also written, in his 1757 *A Philosophical Enquiry into the Origin of our Ideas of the Sublime and Beautiful* that 'There is no spectacle we so eagerly pursue, as that of some uncommon and grievous calamity'.) Although others (such as Thomas Paine (1737–1809) in *The Rights of Man*) still vigorously supported the Revolution and called for universal suffrage and the sovereignty of the people in England, many previously sympathetic to the radical ideas espoused in France now turned away from them. The 'independence of spirit' of which Sir Thomas spoke so scathingly had come to be seen as a threat to the social and political order. Sir Thomas may well be one of those wealthy citizens still terrified by the memory of the Gordon Riots in London in 1780, in which about three hundred people were killed and more damage inflicted on the fabric of London than was to occur in Paris in 1789. The issue at stake in 1780 was religion, but underlying that were tensions about the place of belief in the social world.

The reality of the social order of England, and other European countries at the end of the eighteenth century, was one which was increasingly unlikely to accept without question aristocratic or absolutist authority. This was not because the English, or Europeans, had become, in individual terms, significantly richer or more powerful. Populations were still subject to widespread starvation if harvests failed (for example in the years immediately preceding the Revolution in France), life expectancy was only about 40 years and infant mortality rates remained high. It is the case that by 1800 increasing numbers of people had come to live in towns, where houses were more often built of brick and where chances of schooling were greater than in rural areas, but some of the best-known institutions of eighteenth-century England – for example the establishment of Sir Thomas Coram's home for orphan children in London – came about as a reaction to terrible poverty rather than as a result of generalized social prosperity.

It was not so much the material conditions of life that had changed in the centuries since the Reformation as the sense that individuals had developed of their place in society and their relationship to it. The great thread of events and rethinking of the relationship of men and women to the world which began in the Reformation and continued in the Enlightenment had allowed people to consider the possibility of both understanding and changing the world in which they lived. With this went a rethinking of attitudes to Nature, which expressed itself in great works of classification (for example, the work of the man described as the Father of Taxonomy, the Swede Carl Linnaeus (1707–78)) and the changes in agriculture which eventually led to a more systematic use of land and natural resources. This thread of changed ideas – which included a rethinking not just of the relationship of people to the world but also of the relationship of people to each other – did not occur in similar ways throughout Europe, but by 1800 many of the ideas which we think of as part of the 'modern' world were in place in most parts of Europe and amongst that minority of people for whom existence was more than just a day-to-day struggle for survival. The first of these ideas was a refusal to accept absolutist political power: the degrees to which this refusal was put into practice differed throughout Europe but the idea was there; for example in 1812 the city of Cadiz produced the first Spanish constitution. Second, the idea of the formal equality of all human beings had taken root in the European mind. Years were to pass before this idea was to be fully implemented in formal politics, but the eighteenth century had established – and enshrined in constitutions – that 'all men are created equal'. (It was not until 1861 that the serfs were emancipated in Russia and 1865 when slavery was abolished in the United States.) Finally, a distinction had been made between faith and reason: religion was still hugely important as a source of social morality but the ability of the Christian religion to explain all aspects of the world was no longer generally held in intellectual circles. Europe, by 1800, no longer burnt witches and had been introduced to the possibility of human equality.

The conceptual leaps which Europe had taken by 1800 are best summed up in Mary Shelley's novel *Frankenstein*, in which Shelley encapsulates all those debates about power, reason, science and gender which had been part of the eighteenth century and were to be so significant a part of the centuries to come. In his desire to create a human being, Frankenstein steps beyond the limits of the 'natural' world. In using science and knowledge for his own purposes Frankenstein becomes, as the subtitle of the novel suggests, the 'modern Prometheus'. Empowered by reason, a true child of the Enlightenment, Frankenstein acknowledges no other authority than his own and no other importance except his own project. As a comment on the negative possibilities of the Enlightenment, *Frankenstein* remains the most powerful text yet written, but it is also the most vivid prophecy of the problems which were to come in the next two centuries, in which new forms of production unleashed on the world both new riches and new forms of social conflict and degradation.

Chapter 3

The Technological Revolution

1707   Act of Union between England and Scotland
1738   Publication of *A Treatise on Human Nature* by David Hume
1769   James Watt defines the principle of steam power
1799/   The Combination Acts curtail the organization of workers'
1800   unions
1807   Publication of Hegel's *The Phenomenology of Mind*
1829   Stephenson demonstrates the possible use of the railway
          engine
1834   The deportation of the Tolpuddle Martyrs to Australia
1846–50 The Irish Potato Famine
1851   Publication of Henry Mayhew's *London Labour and London Poor*
1859   Publication of Charles Darwin's *On the Origin of Species*
1867   Publication of the first volume of *Das Kapital* by Karl Marx
1870–71 The Paris Commune
1907   The manufacture of the first Ford motor car

The great Scottish philosopher David Hume (1711–76) remarked in his *Treatise on Human Nature* (written in 1738) that 'Reason is, and ought only to be, the servant of the passions.' The eighteenth and the nineteenth centuries were to show numerous examples of occasions when individuals used their reason to solve problems arising from both intense, if not passionate, curiosity about the world and deeply held convictions about necessary changes in the ordering of the social and political spheres. The success of this use of reason, particularly in the sphere of the problems of the material world, was to make the nineteenth century a century of unprecedented technological change: a century in which the lives of ordinary citizens were to be transformed with a speed and a radicalism never before seen. If we take the Europe of 1500 and the Europe of 1800 we find that, for a great number of Europe's citizens, everyday life would be very similar and instantly recognizable. Life would be lived within limited geographical boundaries, survival itself dependent on the success or failure of the harvest, and the organization of everyday existence dictated by natural light and the seasons. But, by 1900, many of Europe's citizens would be living in towns, and living lives regulated by the clock and imposed timetables of work. People – particularly in parts of northern Europe – could travel with relative ease by railways and had perhaps seen the great exhibitions which demonstrated the links between their country and other, distant, ones. The greatest revolution that the world has ever known was in process in Russia and the ideas and doctrines that were to shape the world in which we live had been defined and articulated. By 1900, people throughout much of Europe had come to recognize the term 'socialism', and the authority to which many people looked was no longer a fixed one of a local church or a landlord but that of an institution such as a trade union, a political party or an interest group. All this has been created in the course of the nineteenth century.

The question of how this transformation came about is in part a continuation of the question raised in the previous chapter about the rise of capitalism. But – and very emphatically – capitalism and industrial society are not the same thing and the capitalism of the sixteenth and seventeenth centuries did not bring with it the technological transformation of the late eighteenth and nineteenth centuries. The rise of capitalism in Europe was due to a number of factors, but amongst those factors was the very important political fragmentation of Europe throughout the medieval period. The countries of Europe were not centralized around a monarch (a brief glance at the history of most European monarchies from the twelfth century onwards will demonstrate that monarchies were unstable rather than anything else), and this provided a social space for the growth of power – and wealth – external to the monarchy. Within this social space, energetic individuals were able to pursue their economic interests, with perhaps a wary eye on the envy of the monarch for individual wealth. The Protestant Reformation, and the subsequent decline in the authority of the papacy on matters related to the making and spending of money, much increased this entrepreneurial activity, but for many recent writers on the subject (for example Henry Kamen), what was crucial about the new attitude to the making of money was not Protestant, particularly Calvinist, beliefs, but the refugee status of many individual Calvinists.[1] Driven out of their countries of origin by religious intolerance and the high taxation of Catholic, Counter-Reformation states, these refugees forged their commitment to the making of capital out of the bitter experience of exile and marginalization.

The capitalism of the seventeenth, eighteenth and early nine-teenth centuries in Europe, which saw the beginning of the tech-nological revolution, was anarchic in form. It was unlike the later form of capitalism, that is, managed capitalism, which was to prevail from the middle of the nineteenth century until the late twentieth century. This initial form of capitalism can be described as anarchic because there was little or no intervention in the activities of indi-vidual entrepreneurs by either organized labour or the state. Small, virtually domestic workshops existed throughout Europe and people moved between places of work with a mobility of both place of residence and nature of employment which would become rare by the late nineteenth century. Interested individuals, people with little formal training in industry or manufacture would busy themselves with ideas about products, and these were often produced out of the domestic space. Typical, indeed prototypical, of this attitude to manufacture was the work produced by the members of the Lunar Society of Birmingham. Jenny Uglow has written of these 'Lunar Men' and drawn a rich and vivid picture of their vitality and their fascination with ideas.[2] Amongst the members of this group were ten men who were to become Fellows of the Royal Society, including Erasmus Darwin (the grandfather of Charles Darwin, the pioneer of evolution), Joseph Priestley, James Watt and Josiah Wedgwood. As Jenny Uglow points out, these men were largely Nonconformists and provincials, people brought up outside London and without a uni-versity education. She quotes the words of Joseph Priestley, who remarked that: 'We were united by a common love of science, which we thought sufficient to bring together persons of all distinctions.'[3]

Here, in one eighteenth-century group, albeit a group which was to have a considerable impact on both manufacture and science in Britain of the late eighteenth century, was the Enlightenment at work. The members of the Lunar Society did not meet to make money, or to think about things to make which might make money, but the many results of their meetings contributed to revolutionary changes in forms of power, manufacture and transport which were to underpin the making of large fortunes. Nor was Birmingham the only location for groups such as these. In other parts of Britain and Europe other men (and this was almost always the case) met to talk about the possibilities of science, again with little initial interest in the potential of science for the making of profit. As E.J. Hobsbawm has pointed out, the list of great scientists before 1750 is largely confined to France, Germany, Britain, Switzerland and Italy, but after that date 'the universe of science widened to embrace countries and peoples which had hitherto made only the smallest contributions to it.'[4] The eighteenth-century interest in exploration and the investigation of the globe provoked a similar interest in the natural history and making of that world. Alexander von Humboldt (1769–1859), the German author of *Kosmos*, typifies this determined enquiry into both the geography of the world and its social and physical reality.

The ordinary citizen of Europe of 1800 might, therefore, have been living in ways which were similar to his or her ancestor in the sixteenth century but, for that section of the population able and determined to take part in the investigation of the world, the frontiers of knowledge had taken a dramatic leap in the seventeenth and eighteenth centuries. Formal literacy was no bar to participation in this activity (James Watt, the inventor of the modern steam engine could neither read nor write) and neither was it necessary to have had a formal education or membership of a dedicated professional society. Napoleon was to establish institutions of higher learning for the study of science and administration (*Ecole Normale Supérieure* in 1794 and the *Ecole Polytechnique* in 1795), and these institutions were to be copied in other parts of Europe, with the exception of Britain. But these institutions came at the end of two centuries in which the boundaries both between what we now know as disciplines and between the world of research and the everyday world were far more fluid than they are today, or were to become in the nineteenth century. Certain forms of investigation, for example mathematics, had a specialist knowledge which was not widely or instantly accessible, but in other areas people came to specific subjects and forms of investigation through a general curiosity or a sense of a problem which needed to be solved. The modern understanding and experience of specialist knowledge – and indeed of living in a society in which the technology is entirely inaccessible to the informed or curious layperson – was not part of the eighteenth century.

The comparative absence of institutionalized forums of knowledge in the seventeenth and the eighteenth centuries allowed participation in the general area of science by those people, especially women, who would be excluded as the nineteenth century saw the gradual institutionalization of knowledge. (One of the best such examples of a woman who played a considerable part in scientific research in the early nineteenth century was Ada Byron (1815–52), the daughter of Lord Byron. Ada Byron was taught mathematics by Mary Somerville and played a crucial part in the making of the first 'analytical engine', the predecessor of the modern computer.) But in the nineteenth century, women throughout Europe had to demand access to the institutions of science and to universities. This was not just for reasons of democratic access but also because these institutions had become virtually the only places in which research, both scientific and technological, was being carried out. Nevertheless, in general, the participation of women in science in the seventeenth and eighteenth centuries was largely that of observation and shared, supportive engagement in the scientific household. In certain cases, however, the education of women was considered to be as important as that of men, and Uglow writes of her Lunar Men as committed to the education of women. Yet at the same time there was a general cultural assumption that women would become wives and mothers, and the difference between the sexes was about a 'natural' and complementary world, in which women and men had different kinds of competence and different kinds of understanding. Challenging that assumption was to become one of the major planks of feminism.

The first major challenge to gendered assumptions about science and knowledge and existing ideas about the nature of women and men came from the extraordinary mother and daughter, Mary Wollstonecraft (1759–97) and Mary Shelley (1797–1851). Apart from the contents of the two best-known works of the women, Wollstonecraft's *A Vindication of the Rights of Woman* and Shelley's *Frankenstein*, what is remarkable about these women is that although Mary Wollstonecraft came from a modest background, her experience (and that of her daughter) embraced many of the social changes and social events of the late eighteenth and early nineteenth centuries. Mary Wollstonecraft was born in 1759 to parents whose social situation was potentially secure (in that her grandfather had amassed some wealth by taking the radical step of transforming his weaving business from a cottage industry into a factory system in which pieceworkers were employed by masters) but rendered insecure by the death of her father. When Mary Wollstonecraft's father died he left nothing to her, her sex and her place in the family effectively disinherited her. Here, in one biography, albeit of a woman who was to become known as the Mother of Modern Feminism, was encapsulated much which was characteristic of eighteenth-century

England: an ongoing transformation of the workplace, a social structure sufficiently open enough for individuals to make considerable amounts of money, alongside the total absence of any form of generally provided state welfare and a social assumption which generally considered boys and men to be more important than girls and women. The essential characteristic of girls and women was taken to be that of dependence: they did not have to be provided for because it was assumed that men (fathers, brothers, husbands, other male relatives) would take care of them. In the case of Mary Wollstonecraft – as it was for millions of other women – this assumption was not matched by reality, and it was an aspect of the social world which Mary was to challenge.

For most of her adult life Mary Wollstonecraft had to do what millions of other women have always had to do: earn a living. But again she did so in ways which were characteristic of her times, in that some of the work which she undertook was unpaid (the care of sick relatives) whilst other forms of work were paid (although the work she provided in a school was run essentially through her household). Equally characteristic of her times – though a less general experience – was the contact which she had with the Dissenters, people whose refusal to acknowledge the basic teaching of the Church of England barred them from the universities of Oxford and Cambridge. (This refusal they turned to advantage for they developed their own institutions of learning throughout England in which they taught the 'new' subjects of history, economics and science.) From these diverse contacts and experiences, including European travel which included a stay in post-Revolutionary France, came *A Vindication of the Rights of Woman*, a book that was to challenge the world that Mary had known. One of its most passionate themes was that of the financial dependence of women on men; Mary Wollstonecraft was the first to use the term 'legal prostitution' to describe marriage and she argued that without financial independence women could never act as free moral agents. Her own life ended giving birth to her daughter Mary, a woman who, at the age of 19 was to write *Frankenstein*, published in 1818 and probably the most radical examination of the arrogance of science that has ever been written. Yet like her mother, Mary Shelley was to suffer the fate of many women of her generation: the awful perils of childbirth and the precarious existence of young children. Although Mary Shelley survived childbirth, three of her four children died in infancy and her surviving son spent much of his life attempting to secure a livelihood for himself and his mother. These histories – of just one family over a period of about fifty years – tell us much of both the ordinary precariousness of existence of the early nineteenth century and yet at the same time the wealth and openness of social networks.

Mary Wollstonecraft had demanded that women be given the same education as men and the same opportunities for earning a living. That wish was to be granted, less by any agreed social policy than by the transformation of the social organization of industry and what we call the Industrial Revolution. The origins of Mary Wollstonecraft's ideas lie in Dissent, the values of the French Revolution and her own experiences as a marginalized daughter whereas the origins of the Industrial Revolution lie in technological achievements and new ideas about how to organize production. The relationship between these two social phenomena – one a highly individual and extraordinary author and the other a set of changes that affected the lives of millions of people – is distant if not non-existent and it would invoke highly deterministic theories about the origin of ideas to assume a close relationship. Nevertheless, what we can observe are the many connections that existed between various individuals who, at the beginning of the nineteenth century, saw the emergence of a new form of society. For example, Thomas Malthus (1766–1834) wrote his famous *An Essay on the Principle of Population* (which argued that without regulation of family size, famine and poverty would result) in direct opposition to the ideas of Rousseau and William Godwin, the husband of Mary Wollstonecraft. But once the Industrial Revolution had taken place (and of course it went on taking place for decades rather than arriving in a complete form in one year), the ideas of Mary Wollstonecraft about the equality of the sexes started to take root in the new circumstances of what had become an industrial, rather than an agrarian, society. In this new society the majority of women needed to work quite as much as men but the terms and conditions on which they participated in this new labour market were dictated by expectations of female dependence on men, and the essential lower monetary value placed on women's work. Despite the fact that, in England, women (largely unmarried, childless women) were the first workers in the new factories of the cotton mills of Lancashire, these women worked in a paternalistic culture. The historian Barbara Taylor has charted the history of women in the early days of the Industrial Revolution, an account which matches E.P. Thompson's *The Making of the English Working*

Class in its innovatory brilliance, and records the remarks of one woman worker, that 'the men are as bad as their masters'.[5]

The men – in this case the fellow workers in the factories but equally possibly the fellow workers in mines – worked with the assumption that a woman's place was in the home and that it was the lot of men to provide for women and children. The idea of the 'family wage' took root throughout Europe in the nineteenth century and it has taken almost two hundred years for this idea to be effectively challenged. For most working-class men, again across Europe, there was no wish for women to be part of the Industrial Revolution. Women should, and did, work in the home, or, as was equally frequently the case, in the homes of others as servants of various status. What the Industrial Revolution did to much of northern Europe was to create a new urban working class, living in the great new cities of Manchester, Birmingham, Lille, Lyons and Hamburg. But this new class was made up of the children of people who had worked on the land and whose ideas about the sexual division of labour did not change dramatically as their place of residence and form of employment changed. Men and women went to work in the new cities because in the new cities there was the promise of work which had one hugely important difference from work on the land: it was not seasonal. Work on the land had always included long periods in which no work could be done, and no work done meant no income. But factories, lit by gas and protected from the elements, could work all year round, and work in ways dictated by the clock rather than the seasons. This new arrangement of work promised (although it did not always fulfil this promise because of the uncertainties of largely unregulated markets) a year-long income and was thus immensely preferable to a way of life which lurched between provision and scarcity.

By the beginning of the nineteenth century the cotton mills of Britain provided evidence of the possibilities of organizing production in factories: by 1833 one and a half million people were employed either directly or indirectly in the manufacture of cotton. 'King Cotton' as it was described at the time was the basis of the Industrial Revolution and the legislation passed in Britain in the first half of the nineteenth century and collectively known as the Factory Acts was primarily directed at the workplace conditions of the cotton mills. The Acts affected other industries (for example mining), but at this period there was no other industry which employed so many people or which had such a transforming effect on the towns of the north-west of England. Other industries developed, both in England and elsewhere, for example brewing in Ireland, but even as this occurred it was still the case that large parts of Europe remained predominantly agricultural and were not to become industrial societies until well into the twentieth century. What industrialization brought with it, apart from appalling urban squalor, was a reordering of the social world, and the emergence of what was to become a self-conscious and organized working class. The term 'working class' is itself somewhat problematic, in that it seems to suggest that prior to the nineteenth century the majority of the European population was neither 'working' nor a 'class'. That was clearly not the case, but the difference that emerged in the nineteenth century was that of an organized working class, a class which did not simply respond to circumstances (as the urban poor had demonstrated that they were more than able to at the time of the French Revolution), but which attempted to change and direct circumstance.

From the last years of the eighteenth century there had been attempts, in both Britain and elsewhere, by groups of labourers to organize themselves and through this to put their case for better pay or improved conditions of work. In Britain this idea had been met by deep disapproval by those in power; the Combination Acts of 1799 and 1800 hampered the growth of trade unions for two generations and the disapproval reached particularly savage points when seventeen men, accused of being Luddites, were executed in 1813 after a trial at York and again, in 1834, when six Dorset labourers in a small village called Tolpuddle were deported to Australia for trying to form an agricultural workers' union. In these instances what we see at the beginning of the nineteenth century is a combination of both the considerable social changes produced by technological change and the reorganization of sections of industry together with the determination of many governments and those in power to refuse to recognize the impact of those changes. By 1850 the British government had had to recognize that the country had changed, and was still changing, and that the structures adequate for the direction of a largely agricultural country were no longer sufficient to maintain a new form of economy and – for many of the population – a new way of life. Remarkable amongst the changes that had taken place since 1800 were alliances between new social groups and the voicing of ideas about the organization of society which would have been irrelevant to previous centuries.

Most significant amongst the new alliances formed in the nineteenth century – and an alliance formed out of the new classes of industrial society – was that between middle-class reformers and radicals and the working class. Philanthropy was not an invention of the nineteenth century: throughout Europe there were long traditions of assistance of various kinds to the poor, the homeless and the sick. But the scale of the urban misery of the nineteenth century, spectacular in the very cities where the rich lived, inspired a new way of thinking about the social divisions between the classes. In western Europe many people came to the conclusion that urban want and deprivation could no longer be met by individual acts of charity and concern. Poverty in the countryside was less immediately visible than in the towns; equally, poverty in the countryside was less likely to impinge on the experiences of the wealthy. The onset of the terrible famines of the nineteenth century – amongst which the Irish Potato Famine of 1846–50 stands out as the most cataclasmic – could be put down to the vagaries of nature and natural disaster; disease, overcrowding and poverty in London or Manchester could not. Indeed, Manchester provides an example of different, but equally impassioned, reactions and remedies to nineteenth-century urban want.

The two writers who are best known for their accounts of Manchester in the first half of the nineteenth century are Elizabeth Gaskell (1810–65) and Friedrich Engels (1820–95), the first the wife of a Unitarian minister and the second the socialist writer, himself supported by the profits of manufacturing industry. But in their different ways they shared a common concern, and a passionate response, to the conditions of life which they found in Manchester in the 1840s, or the 'hungry forties' as they have been described. Here, in his *The Condition of the Working Class in England*, Engels describes a scene in Manchester, in a district not far from the middle-class drawing room of Elizabeth Gaskell:

> The race that lives in these ruinous cottages behind broken windows, mended with oilskin, sprung doors, and rotten doorposts, or in dark, wet cellars, in measureless filth and stench, in this atmosphere penned as if with a purpose, this race must really have reached the lowest stage of humanity ... in each of these pens, containing at most two rooms, a garret and perhaps a cellar, on the average twenty human beings live.[6]

But, for Engels, the 'human beings', although pictured with compassion, have no names and no identity: they are products of certain social forces, even if they are products to be helped and given succour. For Elizabeth Gaskell, the people in these hovels have names, stories, pasts. Writing in her novel *Mary Barton* she speaks of our social reactions to poverty and want:

> The actions of the uneducated seem to me typified in those of Frankenstein, that monster of many human qualities, ungifted with a soul, a knowledge of the difference between good and evil. The people rise up to life; they irritate us, they terrify us, and we become their enemies. Then, in the sorrowful moment of our triumphant power, their eyes gaze on us with a mute reproach. Why have we made them what they are; a powerful monster, yet without the inner means for peace and happiness? John Barton became a Chartist, a Communist, all that is commonly called wild and visionary. Ay! But being visionary is something. It shows a soul, a being not altogether sensual; a creature who looks forward for others, if not for himself.[7]

Elizabeth Gaskell portrays, in *Mary Barton*, the character John Barton driven to murder by the needs of his family, and the slow death, through starvation, of one of his children. As critics have pointed out, Elizabeth Gaskell could not bring herself to vindicate John Barton entirely, nor could she accept social fury as a means of changing the social relations which created poverty. But what she did understand, and convey in both *Mary Barton* and her other 'condition of England' novel, *North and South*, was the connection between the wealth of the rich and the want of the poor. As she points out in *Mary Barton*, even in times of hardship the carriages of the rich roll along the street, the children of the rich do not beg on the streets. Equally, as the extract above indicates, she has a sense of the way in which the social world is created: the reference to Frankenstein, the father of an artificially created human being with energy but no conscience, suggests the ways in which she wished to encourage her readers to think not just of the actual human misery of the Industrial Revolution but equally of the causes of it. In the extract above, Elizabeth Gaskell merges the character of Frankenstein (the maker of the monster – or the Creature as he is referred to in Mary Shelley's novel) and the monster himself. But the merging is interesting because it suggests that neither Frankenstein himself nor the Creature has a conscience: those who have created the exploitation and human misery of industrial society have no more conscience and capacity for human concern than the system itself.

Elizabeth Gaskell, in both *Mary Barton* and *North and South*, is a writer who, in the conclusions of her novels, seeks for reconciliation between individuals and indeed between classes. Engels had no such project and in the two writers we see set out much of the political history of the nineteenth and twentieth centuries. When Elizabeth Gaskell writes that John Barton has become a 'Communist', she refers not to later understandings of this term (those very explicitly associated with Marx and Engels) but with earlier connotations, related to the advocacy of mutually supportive communities such as that expressed in the work of Robert Owen (1771–1858), the founder of the New Lanark Mills. Gaskell speaks for the maintenance of social hierarchy; she has no wish to eradicate social distinctions, but what she very emphatically does want to do is to end a situation in which the poor and the powerless are given no chance of adequate support or any hope of a viable existence, an existence in which there is the expectation of education and a reasonable security.

This is to become the agenda of social reformers throughout Europe in the nineteenth century: slowly, increasing numbers of people come to accept that there is a collective social responsibility for the poor, the sick, the aged and the infirm. We can trace, throughout the nineteenth century, a tradition of growing strength and authority which advocated social reform and was prepared to accept the taxing of the better off to provide for the support of the poor. Nor did fiction provide the only form of inspiration; Engels was one of the first to write documentary accounts of urban need (although his *The Condition of the Working Class in England* was not published in Britain until 1892), but other writers, for example Henry Mayhew (1812–87) in his *London Labour and London Poor* of 1851, provided equally compelling accounts of the circumstances of the urban poor. (In 1850, for example, it was estimated that there were more brothels in London than there were schools and charities put together.[8]) Britain, in common with France, Germany and the Scandinavian countries, had developed by the end of the nineteenth century a state infrastructure – slight and woefully inadequate though it might now appear – to support the needy.

At the same time as a degree of state responsibility for its citizens emerged in Europe it was equally the case that the arguments put by

Engels in 1844 had continuing vitality and continuing appeal. Thus within states that were developing different degrees of state intervention there also existed powerful organizations and influential ideas which advocated far more radical solutions than that of what was essentially an elementary welfare state. These ideas, of socialists, some trade unions and the Communist Party, were born out of the same experiences as those of the social reformers but emerged from different theoretical traditions. Engels, and even more his great collaborator Karl Marx (1818–83), were inspired not only by human sympathy but also by the work of political economists and philosophers. In the case of Marx, two influences stand out. First, the writing of the economist Ricardo (1772–1823) who had pointed out, in his book *Principles of Political Economy and Taxation* (1817) that the price of goods was determined by the value of labour. Second was the German philosopher Georg Friedrich Hegel (1770–1831), the author of *The Phenomenology of Mind* (1807), a work described by Marx as the 'true birthplace and secret of his philosophy'.[9] This description belies those understandings of Marx that associate him only with the form of state socialism later to emerge in eastern Europe; Marx's intellectual heritage was the European Enlightenment and a constant commitment to the idea that the social world could be not just understood but also changed. In an important sense Marx took up Kant's definitive assertion of the value of the Enlightenment – 'dare to know' – and suggested that once we knew, we could also act on that knowledge.

What Marx was to take from Hegel, and make his own, was the idea of the relationship between a master and a slave, a relationship which at first appears to be static and defined by the power of the one and the powerlessness of the other but is in fact deeply unstable. Between the master and the slave there is what Hegel described as a 'dialectic', a relationship in which the slave, through his work, produces change in the world and in doing so changes his relationship with his master. What the idea allows is the dynamic of human relationships, both collective and individual and it is this dynamic which Marx was to make the core of his social theory and account of the social world. But, and it is a very important qualification, Marx was not the first person to be interested in the dynamics of social change. What made Marx's theory of the social world so radical was his assertion (in his *The German Ideology* of 1846) that 'Consciousness does not determine life, but life determines consciousness.' That sentence is the summary of Marx's ideas in that context: in the same passage he sets out the idea more fully:

In direct contrast to German philosophy, which descends from heaven to earth, here we ascend from earth to heaven. That is to say, we do not set out from what men say, imagine, conceive, nor from men as narrated, thought of, imagined, conceived, in order to arrive at men in the flesh. We set out from real, active men, and on the basis of their real life-process we demonstrate the development of the ideological reflexes and echoes of this life-process. ... Morality, religion, metaphysics and all the rest of ideology and their corresponding forms of consciousness no longer seem to be independent. They have no history or development. Rather, men who develop their material production and their material relationships alter their thinking and the products of their thinking along with their real existence.[10]

Not even the most determined opponent of Marx's views could contest that in the nineteenth century material production altered. The evidence was everywhere throughout Europe. Factory chimneys appeared, and towns and cities were made out of what had previously been villages: the ideas of the metropolitan and the cosmopolitan arrived on the European scene. The manufacture of goods and services was vastly accelerated by new forms and social relations of production, the organization of factory production, as much as a new technology, gave to production a mechanized and routine quality. Individual craft workers did not disappear but their work – in the making, for example, of clothes or furniture – came to be purchased only by the rich; by the end of the twentieth century the term 'hand-made' was to indicate a special, rare and probably costly object. Thus what is not in contention in the accounts by either Marx or Engels of the new 'machine age' of the nineteenth century is the accuracy of their recognition of a changed form of production. What is more contentious, and what remains the crucial question for all theories of society (and the politics which accompany them) is the extent to which Marx's assumption that 'consciousness does not determine life, but life determines consciousness' remains useful and accurate.

Marx's theory of society, that the labour of the proletariat is used, within capitalism, to create the wealth of the bourgeoisie, is, at first sight, a vivid, but perhaps not wildly exaggerated, account of nineteenth (and indeed twentieth) century social relations. A first glance at nineteenth-century Europe shows a continent in which vast fortunes were made out of industry for a few individuals, whilst much of the population lived in various degrees of want and deprivation. Although the nineteenth century saw a gradual improvement in living standards (and such measurements of social health as rates of infant mortality and life expectancy), life remained, for many people, hideously insecure. Illness and unemployment could destroy, almost overnight, any modicum of individual comfort that existed, and telling statistics (such as the revelation that many British men, examined for possible military service at the time of the Boer War, from 1899 to 1902, were simply unfit to fight) demonstrated the parlous level of general health. That dramatic collective example of a nation's ill health can be equalled by the example of the family of the Brontë sisters, most famously Anne (1820–49), Charlotte (1816–55) and Emily (1818–1848). Of seven children born into a degree of middle-class security not one child lived beyond the age of 40. Although this family has acquired lasting fame for the work of its members, its experience of a history of early deaths is not exceptional. The diseases that killed the Brontë children (tuberculosis and various forms of water-borne infections) did not disappear until public health improved in the twentieth century. The first decades of industrialization suggest that Marx's assumption that the proletariat would become 'impoverished' through this new social world was largely correct.

Marx assumed, however, two aspects of social life which did not lead to that victory of the proletariat which he considered to be likely, if not inevitable. The first was that although the term 'proletariat' is entirely accurate in describing the relation of the vast majority of the population to paid work (put bluntly, if we do not work, for money, then we do not eat), there were, and are, considerable degrees of difference between the various workers of any society. There are, as sociologists have always observed, 'middle-class' workers, 'professionals' and highly skilled manual workers. We do not enter that world of paid work with the same skills, the same attitudes and the same aspirations. The sociological terms 'middle class' and 'working class' are in no sense the same as Marx's terms 'bourgeoisie' and 'proletariat' (although in cultural terms there has come to be some similarity of meaning), but what both include are individuals whose views do not necessarily reflect those politics which Marx assumed to be the case. The ranks of those industrialists who made fortunes in the nineteenth and twentieth centuries are not cluttered with evidence of philanthropy (although there were exceptions such as the British Rowntree family), and, in general, the wealthy throughout Europe worked for state policies that would protect their wealth. But amongst other social groups there were those who worked for general social improvement (be they famous hospital reformers or unknown village schoolteachers) just as much as there were individuals who believed passionately in the existence of trade unions and the rights of the poor to political enfranchisement. Sections of the middle class in countries across Europe could show degrees of social altruism which had an important impact on changing state policies towards the needy. Thus in some European countries the taking over by the proletariat of the state has been postponed, if not made unlikely, by active attempts to question those social divisions which ensured the hardship of the many for the privileges of the few.

A second factor which contributed to the failure of proletarian revolutions in Europe was the unwillingness of the proletariat as a whole to take part in radical social movements. Many European countries had active communist parties from the end of the nineteenth century onwards and these parties played crucial roles in historical events such as the Paris Commune of 1870–71 and revolutionary protests in Germany in 1918. But for a variety of historical reasons in neither case was the proletariat as a whole mobilized: for Marxists the 'false consciousness' of the proletariat was such as to prefer bourgeois democracy to socialist revolution. The Russian Revolution of 1917 proved the exceptional case of a revolution made from the theoretical work of Marx but brought into being through a rather different understanding of politics. The evolution of a socialist society, which Marx thought would be an inevitable historical process, was given some historical acceleration by the determination of the leaders of the Russian Revolution, notably Lenin (1870–1924) and Trotsky (1879–1940), to force the rate of historical change through the leadership of a disciplined and centralized party. Britain, by the end of the nineteenth century, had significant groups of people working together to bring about radical social change, but in the case of Britain much of this energy was channelled into existing political structures, notably the idea of what has become known as 'Westminster democracy', the state run by free elections, contested by a small number of political parties. The willingness of the British working class to participate in Westminster democracy resulted in the establishment of the Labour Party and eventually the first Labour government, led by Ramsay MacDonald, in 1924.

This model of political change, and political agency, although it is one which the West takes for granted as the definitive organization of western politics, did not come into being without fierce contest throughout the nineteenth century. In Britain in 1800 very few people could vote; being able to vote was essentially a property qualification, available only to men. By 1900 almost all British men could vote, although all women did not get the vote until 1929. (Childhood and childishness was thought to last longer in women: British women over 30 were given the vote in 1919, women over the age of 21 were enfranchised in 1929). So, by the end of the nineteenth century a set of new relations had emerged in politics, relationships which involved the consent, or at least the collusion, of a section of the population and participation of hitherto excluded classes (and eventually a gender) in the political process. The revolution which Marx had assumed would take place had not occurred and in many ways the twentieth century promised less chance of truly radical social change in Britain than did the end of the nineteenth century.

The reasons for this, and for the absence of socialist revolutions in other European countries, lie in a number of factors, both social and cultural. Historians of the eighteenth century, for example Linda Colley, have suggested that Britons (and after the Act of Union of 1707 it is possible to speak of mainland Britain as a politically united whole) acquired a sense of national identity in the eighteenth century.[11] This 'making of the nation' argument is supported by those who see Britain in the eighteenth and nineteenth centuries as a country in which various symbols of nationhood, for example monarch and Empire, became the organizing structures for a sense of shared identity. Radical social groups – and indeed radical intellectual life – existed side by side with a considerable degree of social support for national social and political institutions. For example, despite her long years of seclusion, Queen Victoria was a genuinely popular figure, not least because she recognized – and frequently pointed this out to her many children – that the monarch had a duty to engage with her subjects. Her grand-daughter, the last tsarina of Russia, somewhat foolishly rejected this advice. The nineteenth-century political writer Walter Bagehot (1826–77), famous for *The English Constitution* of 1867, spoke of 'nation building' as a phenomenon of his age. This sense of creating a national identity can be seen throughout Europe in the various structures and edifices that came into being during this period, all of them to demonstrate the particular genius of a particular nation. Nor were nations the only group glorified; almost every urban centre of any size constructed some kind of building to demonstrate its wealth and glory and the great town halls of northern England were visible evidence of pride in a place and its people.

These symbols of nation and place were not, however, designed to fulfil a merely symbolic function. They were also evidence of one of the other great social characteristics of the nineteenth century: the growth of bureaucracies and the increased organization of daily life. Again, if we return to 1800 we find little intrusion by the organized state into the lives of most people. There were, and had been for centuries, complex administrative arrangements for running certain state functions: the military, the collection of revenue, papers about overseas possessions, all these existed and involved considerable work and expertise. But on a daily basis, for the majority of citizens, there was little legislation that demanded printed records of either existence or participation in everyday life. For example, parents did not have to send their children to school, or be accountable if those children did not attend school. Adults did not have to produce written evidence of participation in paid work or the taxation system. The ownership of a house, or tenancy arrangements, were frequently verbal arrangements, and most citizens had absolutely no claim to legal redress for situations such as eviction or redundancy. As individuals, citizens of Europe in 1800 did not possess the 'paper lives' which have become so much a feature of the present day.

The origin of this apparently relentless need for documentation of the individual arose, at least in part, from the multiplicity of new institutions that were established in the nineteenth century. Industrial society needed literate workers, social reformers fought for better education, health care and public housing, and out of these different demands came various forms of provision. But it was provision which had to be paid for – hence new tax systems – and regulated – hence the need for written evidence of claims and eligibility. As the Industrial Revolution made its mark throughout much of northern Europe so an infrastructure followed which both enlarged the state provision for citizens and at the same time vastly increased the accountability of the citizen to the state. This degree of social control over the lives of individuals has been variously described as 'surveillance', by the French historian Michel Foucault (1926–84) or the 'iron cage' of bureaucracy by Max Weber. To Foucault the characteristic building of the nineteenth century, indeed the building that epitomizes the society in which it is found, is the panopticon, originally a prison building design put forward by the British Utilitarian philosopher Jeremy Bentham (1748–1832). Bentham's building was one in which every cell in a prison could be seen from a central tower, a particularly efficient way of making sure that everyone in the building could be kept under constant watch. Nor was this building design to be used only for prisons: it was equally suitable for hospitals, schools and workshops. In these buildings the lives of the various inmates could be measured and accounted for: order and stability were made more likely and out of what could have been a potentially disorderly and threatening group of inmates came a docile and, most importantly, controllable subject population.

This architecture of order is, to many social theorists, the visible embodiment of the dominating ideas of the nineteenth century, ideas in which concerns for social equality and improvement stood alongside fears of social disorder and social breakdown. Both traditions are omnipresent throughout the nineteenth century: the legions of social reformers alongside the politicians and monarchs ever fearful of social unrest and the overthrow of their own authority. Nor, of course, were these fears groundless: the French once again overthrew their monarchy in 1870 but, in the bloodshed that followed, thousands of Communards were killed or deported. As the centralized state became more powerful (and organized more aspects of daily life), so its capacity for revenge on those who challenged its authority became more lethal. The kind of virtually unarmed protest which had played such an important part in the years immediately prior to the first French Revolution became impossible as states learnt to protect themselves with new forms of policing.

Indeed, the function of 'policing' became one of the great new professions of the nineteenth century. States had had forms of policing, both clandestine and public, for centuries, but what was distinctive about the policing that emerged in the nineteenth century was its extent and its competence. Britain, in common with other European powers, notably France, the Netherlands and Belgium, had an empire to run and did so with extraordinary success even though this was an age before telephone and wireless communication. The populations subject to the European powers in the nineteenth century, without sophisticated armaments and largely illiterate, were no match for Europeans with systems of political and social control and military expertise to back up their rule in these conquered territories. What had originally been trading relations (for example in the case of the British presence in India) became, by the nineteenth century, the political and cultural subordination of ancient nations and peoples. Britain, in common with the other European colonial powers of the nineteenth century, explained its intervention in the domestic politics of subject nations with a mixture of self-interest and the justification of the 'improvement' of the dominated by the dominators. Christian missionaries of various denominations took the Christian gospels to people with complex religious systems of their own. What was to emerge out of the various meetings of cultures was an exchange of values and ideas which was often, but not exclusively, one sided and enforced with various degrees of severity. But by the beginning of the twentieth century those parts of the globe which had been claimed for the British Empire were asking for their nations and lands to be returned to their original inhabitants. Decolonization was to be a slow, tortuous and still incomplete process of the twentieth and twenty-first centuries, but we can now recognize that at every stage this colonial relationship was contested and opposed.

The making of the British Empire, and other European empires, is a part of the history of Europe in the nineteenth century that united an ancient historical event (the making of empires) with new forms of social relations, those of industrial capitalism. Thus whilst the extraction of valuable goods from a subject people is no new event in history, what was different about the new colonial relations of the nineteenth century was the eventual involvement of the economy of the subject people in the economy of the conquered. The new territories of European empires were not just suppliers of raw materials (even, in the case of the diasporic relations of the slave trade, human labour) but were intended also as markets for the manufactured goods of Europe. In the nineteenth century the unequal economic relations of the global marketplace were established: countries now became 'poor' not because they lacked human or physical resources but because they did not have access to western technology and in particular to manufacturing capacity. Societies and cultures which for generations had provided for themselves now had their material relations overturned by both the social and cultural expectations of Europeans (for example, that it was men who were the primary traders or that all societies were organized in patriarchal nuclear families) and the absence of the primary skills (reading, writing) necessary to run an industrial society. The marketplace, and even more the social relations of the market economy of Europe, put in place a new map of the world. Again, this reflected not so much the extension of trading relations, since these had existed for centuries, as the scale and the nature of these relations.

In the nineteenth-century making of the global economy one of the arguments proposed for the validation of this exercise was that of 'enlightening' and educating those apparently left behind in what was thought of as the progress of civilization. It is thus that in the nineteenth century Britain and Europe first encountered the emergence of the ideas which have since been defined as Social Darwinism. The theories take their name from the study of animal and human evolution, *On the Origin of Species by Means of Natural Selection, or the Preservation of Favoured Races in the Struggle for Life* by Charles Darwin (1809–82), first published in 1859. The book immediately became famous, and contentious, not least because it challenged the biblical explanation of the evolution of man. In suggesting that human beings could trace their ancestry through monkeys, Darwin was thought by his critics to make a mockery of the biblical view that man was created in the image of God. But the impact of Darwin was not to be confined to those who could not abandon the literal reading of the Bible. Karl Marx was so deeply impressed by *On the Origin of the Species* that he offered to dedicate the second volume of *Das Kapital* to Darwin. Darwin, less convinced of Marx's ideas than Marx was of his, declined. Equally, writers on the political right rather than the political left saw in Darwin's work an extraordinarily helpful explanation for the technological poverty of much of Africa and of people anywhere living in poverty: these cultures lacked intellectual competence. Sociobiology and genetics were just two of the intellectual results of Darwin's work; both areas in which valuable as well as straightforwardly ideological work has subsequently been done. Those who read Darwin's work as an account of the intellectual superiority of white men read it as a profoundly 'natural' explanation of the social world. Indeed, for those most convinced by this reading of Darwin, the technologically sophisticated societies of the world had 'evolved' not through changes in social relations (particularly social relations to knowledge) but through the 'natural' intellectual superiority of their inhabitants.

What Darwin gave to the nineteenth century was an account of the evolution of human beings which challenged biblical teachings and affronted many of those committed to essentially ahistorical accounts of human life and relations. For those who interpreted Darwin in terms of the 'survival of the fittest' then all forms of exploitation or conquest were not part of a social process but a natural one. In this account of the world there was simply no point in providing social assistance to the needy, let alone challenging the existence of traditional social relations. The extent to which Darwin remains an intensely political figure can be demonstrated by the fact that his work cannot be taught in some schools in some areas of the United States: the biblical explanation of the origin of the world, and of human beings, is now asserted as a fact, despite the weight of scientific evidence which suggests a contrary explanation.

This latest manifestation of the resistance to science and the possibility of the multiple interpretations of texts is not, and no doubt will not be, the last such manifestation in history. Throughout the nineteenth century it is possible to observe both scientific and technological progress and equally impassioned resistance to it. The first years of the Industrial Revolution were marked by attempts to destroy the machines which threatened the livelihood of workers: 'Luddite' reactions to technology take their name (albeit somewhat unfairly) from these first, failed attempts. In the middle of the nineteenth century various writers in Britain, for example John Ruskin (1819–1900), expressed their dislike of the new industrial world. In *Time and Tide* (1867) Ruskin argued against economic competition and advocated a form of Christian socialism. William Morris (1834–96), with Edward Burne-Jones (1833–98) and Dante Gabriel Rossetti (1828–82), a member of the group which called themselves The Pre-Raphaelite Brotherhood, advocated a return to what they saw as the previous conditions of production, essentially the artisan working to produce hand-made goods. The so-called Gothic Revival in Britain in the nineteenth century, as a result of which the Houses of Parliament were rebuilt in their present Gothic style by the architects Charles Barry (1795–1860) and Auguste Pugin (1812–52), was a product of both a dislike of the results of the new technology and a somewhat selective interpretation of the past, particularly the medieval past. To Ruskin, Morris, Pugin and others, industry and technology had hastened the abolition of community. The German sociologist Ferdinand Tönnies (1855–1936) echoed this view in his *Gemeinschaft und Gesellschaft* (1887) and the theme of the alienation of the individual from the social world of industrial society was further taken up by Emile Durkheim in *The Division of Labour in Society* (published in 1893).

These various degrees of nostalgia for the past (although Durkheim and Tönnies are perhaps less immediately culpable than

Morris and Pugin) might have been contested by many citizens of nineteenth-century Europe, for whom the century had brought quite novel peace, comfort and security. One of the many paradoxes of the nineteenth century is that whilst there is nostalgia for the past (and arguably more nostalgia than in previous societies where the rate of change had not been so rapid), there was also a widespread recognition of both the positive and the negative in the new order. Amongst those negative aspects of the new order were relations between women and men. Indeed, one of the most striking transcultural narratives of the nineteenth century is the portrayal of the destructive human relations that resulted from nineteenth-century norms of femininity and masculinity, in which the social behaviour of women and men was expected to follow a clearly defined path. In his novel *Anna Karenina* Leo Tolstoy (1828–1910) implicitly questioned the impossibility of divorce in nineteenth-century Russia (and he might have added, everywhere else at the same time) and the rigidity of moral codes when faced with the complexity of human experience. In France, Britain and Germany both male and female writers looked at the reality of relations between women and men in their societies and wrote of the often appalling consequences of a social world in which women were given little scope for individual agency – other than in the choice of their marriage partners – and where men were supposed to abide by strict codes of personal conduct. Part of the dominant social code of sexual morality in the nineteenth century – and a code which could be found throughout Europe, was what was described as the sexual 'double standard', a standard in which the sexual behaviour of women was policed far more rigidly than that of men and in which the consequences of rejecting accepted standards of sexual behaviour were, for women, far more significant than was the case for men. The assumptions of the double standard were rooted in norms of heterosexuality. Homosexuality, increasingly marginalized and prosecuted as the nineteenth century went on, was both part of the very making of nineteenth-century masculinity and yet at the same time publicly forbidden. The trial of the writer Oscar Wilde (1854–1900) in 1895 for his homosexual relationship with Lord Alfred Douglas is one of the points in nineteenth-century Britain when homophobic fears became apparent.

Those women who became what sections of Victorian society might have described as 'fallen' were often subject to social ostracism and abandonment. But women themselves fought these definitions and the new technological world offered much to many women. First, medical science gave to women the increased likelihood of surviving, with their children, childbirth. The relief of pain in childbirth, the increased use of antiseptics in midwifery, and in medicine generally, resulted in a drop in the rate of both maternal and infant deaths. The death of Mary Wollstonecraft in childbirth, together with the death in infancy of three of her grandchildren, would have become, by the end of the nineteenth century, significantly less likely. Second, work in the home, and work at home, had for many women started to become less exhausting as manufactured goods – food, clothing – started to become available. Equally, housing with piped water, gas lighting and brick walls did away with some of the squalor that Engels and Elizabeth Gaskell had described in the first half of the nineteenth century. By the end of the nineteenth century the labour of women had become needed in contexts other than those of domestic service or factory work. The infrastructure of technology needed clerical workers and sales staff to service the new industries and the new palaces of consumption. These palaces, be they department stores, or hotels, or theatres, were very often anxious to appeal to women, and women became an important market to sections of manufacturing industry. The urban world gave to many women hitherto unknown possibilities of freedom of movement, possibilities which were now democratically available rather than restricted to the rich and the privileged. In those cases of transparent discrimination in the rights of citizens, women had acquired, by the end of the nineteenth century, experience in collective organization. The successes of campaigns by women in the nineteenth century included changes in property law, the right to a higher education, access to professional training and organized trade union representation.

The technological innovations and changes of the nineteenth century probably had more impact on the lives of ordinary citizens than any other single event in the previous four hundred years. This is not to say that families were made in radically new ways (although people made different kinds of families as the requirement of education made children an economic cost rather than an economic asset) or that people turned their backs on previously held beliefs and behaviour. But it is to suggest that those great cultural and intellectual transformations, the Renaissance, the Reformation and the Enlightenment, whilst significant, made less impact on the daily lives of ordinary citizens than the coming of the machine age and the reorganization of production. At the same time, the degree of organization in society markedly increased: the spontaneous and the unexpected were now not just different events in the social world, they were also often unwelcome and unlikely. The social consequences of this phenomenon – the sense of the loss of the irrational in the modern – was to prove to be a crucial factor in the twentieth century and the point at which the new, general experience of a shared culture made possible by a new technology was to unite with the social ideas inherited from the Enlightenment.

Chapter 4

Contested Modernity

1900   Publication of *The Interpretation of Dreams* by Sigmund Freud

1907   First exhibition of *Les Demoiselles d'Avignon* by Picasso

1914–18 First World War

1917   Russian Revolution

1924   Death of Lenin

1929   Wall Street Crash

1933   Adolf Hitler becomes Chancellor of Germany

1939–45 Second World War

1945   Explosion of nuclear bombs at Hiroshima and Nagasaki

1949   Publication of George Orwell's *1984*

1989   The 'Fall of the Wall': the political collapse of the Soviet Union and its satellite states

For many historians the 'modern' begins in the sixteenth century, when the absolute intellectual authority of the Catholic Church was broken and Europeans began to explore alternative explanations of the world and ways of living in it. As we have seen in earlier chapters, the theory has a good deal to support it. So too does the view that the 'modern' began in 1789: the overthrow of the French monarchy not by the factional politics of the aristocracy but by the determined action of 'the people' can be seen as the beginning of democratic politics in Europe. But the third usual date for the beginning of the 'modern' is 1900, a date which marked not just the beginning of a new century but arguably the emergence of a new understanding about human beings, a new understanding which is generally labelled 'modernism'. It was in 1900 that Sigmund Freud published his *The Interpretation of Dreams*, a book which took the idea of discovery to realms not previously envisaged, the realms of the unknown and the undisclosed within every human being. Seven years later, Pablo Picasso exhibited for the first time his painting *Les Demoiselles d'Avignon*, a painting which deserted all representational

expectations of the literal in favour of the abstract and the inter-
pretative. Narrative painting became the painting, and the way of
portraying the world, of the previous century. These developments
suggest considerable creative energy in the intellectual world of the
early twentieth century; more pessimistically Max Weber was to
remark in 1905 (in the articles which were to become *The Protestant
Ethic and the Spirit of Capitalism*) that the 'rosy blush of the Enlightenment seems to be irretrievably fading'.

Neither Freud nor Picasso was welcomed with open arms by the
worlds in which they lived. Europe in 1900 had become, in some
countries and in some parts of some countries, an industrial society
but it was still a society in which there was deep scepticism about the
avant-garde. Indeed, Europe in 1900 was in many ways a traditional
society: religion and religious observance remained a part of all
European cultures, men retained considerable power, both literal and
symbolic, over women, and social deference – accepting the idea of
social hierarchy – was widely observable. A considerable section of
the European middle class still expected to have servants in their
homes, and in very few of those homes was the education of women,
or the social situation of those servants, of much concern. For that
majority of Europe which was not middle class the material conditions of life had improved in the previous century but unemployment, sickness and old age still brought with them poverty and
hardship. The reports of those middle-class Europeans who took an
interest in the well-being of the poor (for example the Fabians in
England) record the misery of many working-class lives and the
scarcity of both money and material possessions which does not
accord at all with expectations of the interior of a middle class Victorian house or of an ordinary home in 2000. The welfare state had
not arrived in Europe, although individual countries had started to
take small steps towards the idea of state provision.

Whilst the extent of the division between classes remained as
dramatic in 1900 as it had been in 1800, what had changed was the
emergence in Europe of socialist politics and self-conscious and
assertive working-class politics. The class that emerged out of the
European Industrial Revolution was one whose history was made
both by writers from the middle class (the obvious example being
Karl Marx) and by working-class activists whose daily workplace
struggles were now expressed through theories of society and ideas
about universal social change. This was a self-conscious working
class, largely male and largely based in manufacturing industry. The

factories making iron and steel, the coal mines and the shipyards of
Europe were all places where men worked together and formed
together an understanding of the world which was based on the idea
of solidarity in social relations. The social cultures which arose from
these work-based associations were often misogynistic and fiercely
local but what they did do was to provide for large sections of the
population both an effective form of political representation and
protection against the otherwise savage world of industrial capitalism. To read of the workplace conditions of the early twentieth
century in the twenty-first century returns the reader to a world of
danger and dirt. By the end of the twentieth century a great many of
the industries of Europe which had made the European Industrial
Revolution and the European working class would have closed down
in Europe and moved to other parts of the world. But at the beginning of the twentieth century Europe had a primary position in
world manufacturing, a position which was just starting to be
challenged by the United States.

The organization of the industrial working class into trade
unions (people working on the land were to remain largely non-
unionized and with little of the political strength of their urban
counterparts) was not looked upon with great favour by the wealthy
of early-twentieth-century Europe. One of the many important
characteristics of political struggles in Europe in the twentieth century is that although class divisions were marked, the turbulent and
bloody politics of twentieth-century Europe were too complex to be
understood simply in terms of class divisions or class struggles.
Although the Revolution in Russia in 1917 accords with models of
social change in which the working class (or proletariat) seize power
from the wealthy (or bourgeoisie), the political upheavals of twentieth-century Europe, which brought havoc and misery to millions of
people, were struggles about culture as well as about the more
transparent politics of class. E.J. Hobsbawm has pointed out that the
twentieth century is the bloodiest century in all of human history, a
century without parallel in terms of death and destruction. Although
the map of Europe has been changing for the past thousand years,
the rate at which the frontiers and boundaries of Europe changed in
the twentieth century was greater than in any other century. Empires
disappeared – notably the Austro-Hungarian Empire with its claims
of descent from Charlemagne – and new countries emerged. Perhaps
most notably, a great deal of Europe experienced foreign occupation
between 1939 and 1945; the end to the power of Nazi Germany

allowed in its stead the domination of a significant part of Europe by another external power, the Soviet Union.

The questions that confront us at the beginning of the twentieth century are questions about the changing cultures of twentieth-century Europe and the reasons why new ways of looking at the world, in the period after 1900, were regarded so suspiciously and with such concern. Again, it is important to remind ourselves that new ideas, and their capacity to inspire both furious resistance and furious defence, were no new phenomena for Europe. In the previous chapters we saw that the Reformation led to over a hundred years of religious wars in Europe, and the French Revolution created a European politics of intense defensiveness about the invasion of the ideas of the Revolution, quite as much as literal invasion by the French. It is commonplace to picture Europe of the past as a tranquil place, until that tranquillity was shattered by the rise of fascism, but in many parts of Europe that tranquillity was often a distant possibility. A brief glance at the paintings of the late-eighteenth-century Spanish artist Goya, for example, shows in part a bucolic and pastoral world but also a world of death and cruelty – a world in which, as the title of one of Goya's paintings suggests, 'reason' is well and truly asleep. The Enlightenment had allowed much of Europe to 'dare to know' (in Kant's phrase), but daring to know did not inevitably bring with it social peace and harmony. Much of the narrative fiction of the nineteenth century, be it in England, Russia or France, embraces a concept of the new, but the new explored in the nineteenth century is – with one important exception – a new which is largely concerned with the material new. The great exception to this is the exploration in fiction of the possibilities of changes in gender roles: what nineteenth-century writers, be they male or female, saw was the problem of how women and men were to relate to one another and what possible part women could have in a world which wished to confine them, across all classes, to the household. Again, we have seen that this was not actually the case for many working-class women since material circumstance rendered it essential for them to work either in a public workplace or in the homes of others. But the ideal was there, imprinted on the social mind (and indeed the minds of millions of individuals) that a woman's place was in the home and that without this presence the home, the household, would become a place of chaos. Every home, it was widely thought, should have an 'angel in the house'.

To link gender relations with the upheavals of the twentieth century might at first seem perverse and certainly distant from the historical orthodoxy which concentrates on the workings of the economy and its political system. Emphasizing gender relations is not to argue that more conventional factors did not play a crucial part in the history of the twentieth century. But it is to suggest that the fault line, in all European societies, of gender relations contributed to a general uneasiness about social change and the progress (and destination) of 'the new'. Robert Hughes has described the emergence of abstract art in Europe at the beginning of the twentieth century as *The Shock of the New* and equally shocking, for many people, were the ideas about the 'new women' of the late nineteenth century. In Charlotte Brontë's novel *Jane Eyre* (published in 1847), Jane had cried out against her domestic seclusion and expressed her longing for a wider world and a greater social world than that of the household. Jane was eventually to accept domestic life. ('Reader, I married him' was to be the end of Jane's story in much the same way as it was for many of her contemporaries.) But other Janes did not choose – or could not choose – the same resolution. 'New Women', the women so feared by male authors such as Arnold Bennett, D.H. Lawrence and H.G. Wells, started to question the assumption that married life was, for women, the be all and end all of social existence. In the last decade of the nineteenth century and the first years of the twentieth the politics of gender became an important part of cultural politics.

Nowhere was this more clearly apparent than in the lives and in the friendships of the group of people collectively known as the Bloomsbury Group. Although the Group has been widely mocked and derided (not least by the writer George Orwell), amongst its members were two people, Virginia Woolf and John Maynard Keynes, who were to have a definitive impact on twentieth-century culture and politics. Indeed, it is perhaps no exaggeration to say that the lives of millions of us have been directly affected by the economic theories of Keynes. Probably the same universal significance is not true of Woolf, but nevertheless her ideas have played their part in constructing the culture and understanding of the twentieth century. The Bloomsbury Group, formed out of a network of friendships, included (apart from Virginia Woolf and Keynes) the painter Duncan Grant, Vanessa Bell, the sister of Virginia Woolf, the biographer Lytton Strachey and the art critic Roger Fry. There were many other figures – of greater or lesser significance – but the core of the group revolved around the two sisters, Virginia and Vanessa and their husbands, Leonard Woolf and Clive Bell. In one case or another all these figures took part in the most important events of the early twentieth century: as a group they were passionately opposed to the First World War and what they regarded as its insane militarism and nationalism; Leonard and Virginia Woolf were responsible for the first translations of Freud into English; Keynes took part in the making of the Versailles Treaty at the end of the First World War and fiercely opposed the punitive reparations imposed on Germany; and Roger Fry was one of the most influential figures in the bringing of modernism and abstract art to England. Other figures – for example Lytton Strachey – turned their critical gaze on the pieties and certainties of Victorian England: Strachey's *Eminent Victorians* suggested that the apparently great figures of nineteenth-century England were no more than constructions of their age. The past – in the work of Fry and Strachey in particular – was not a sacred place, any more than the nation was to be uncritically defended or praised.

Amongst the Bloomsbury Group there was, therefore, a view of early-twentieth-century culture, and early-twentieth-century Britain, which did not embrace the givens and the certainties of conventional social life. This was apparent in their politics, both personal and more general, and in their attitudes to the social world. What the Group had accepted, to a greater or a lesser extent, was a cluster of beliefs which can be identified throughout Europe at the beginning of the twentieth century and which, in fact, can be traced through pan-European networks and associations. Amongst these beliefs was a profound scepticism about the meaning and importance of nation, together with an equally profound scepticism about rigid definitions of gender. Belief in God was seldom part of the world view of any member of the European avant-garde; in its various forms of anti-clericalism (France) or dislike of the established Church of Anglicanism (England) there was little support for traditional forms of religion. Religion, gender, nation were not to be accepted as givens but were to be regarded critically and often as both hostile to understanding and positively dangerous in their implications. Keynes recognized that the furious nationalism which demanded revenge on Germany in 1918 could only have the most woeful long-term consequences; Woolf asserted the rights of women not just, famously, to a 'room of one's own' but to distance from normative, mainstream – and male – values. But what they all did, either literally or in their work, was to argue that sex did not define sexuality: for the first time in European cultural history a group of people challenged the idea that male and female biology had inevitable social consequences and identities. Again, it is important to recall that gender ambiguity and cross-dressing are all parts of European cultural history. Yet what occurred in the bourgeois drawing rooms of Bloomsbury and the pastoral locations of the Sussex countryside was a self-conscious realization of the possibilities of breaking the link between biological sex and social behaviour. Little wonder, perhaps, that the Bloomsbury Group were sometimes referred to as the Bloomsbury Buggers by the more hostile of their critics: the sexual politics of the majority of the individual members of the Group fell far short of the conventional.

Recent historical accounts of the past have rightly reminded us that writing about the past can make false assumptions about it, and assumptions which depend very much more on what a particular historian might like to have been the case than on what actually was the case. In the 1970s, for example, feminist historians in Britain, Europe and the United States were to reclaim the unwritten history of women. In Sheila Rowbotham's famous book title, women had been 'hidden from history'. Equally, the history of working-class people and people of colour has received less attention than that of those groups and individuals who accord more easily with dominant social expectations. In this context it would be misleading to define the behaviour of the Bloomsbury Group as the only instance of unconventional behaviour in Britain or Europe in the early years of the twentieth century. This was not the case, and throughout the nineteenth century there was a definable bohemian culture in all major European cities which drew on post-Romantic ideas about human relations and the value, above all others, of the creative life. The creation of the 'bohemian' life is a part of nineteenth-century history and the Bloomsbury Group is a part of the continuation of that history in the twentieth century. But what is particular about the history of the Bloomsbury Group is that its history, and its ideas, stood in a very precise relationship to the dominant ideas and events of the day. Bohemian culture has often been outside conventional society, and for many of its members that has been its major attraction. But individual members of Bloomsbury were very much concerned with the world outside its own boundaries, and their involvement was with some of the major ideas and social movements of the twentieth century. Three of those ideas deserve particular attention: about gender roles, colonialism and the role of the state.

Virginia Woolf is well known for her discussion, in *A Room of One's Own* (1929) and *Three Guineas* (1938) of the priority given to the education and the interests of men, just as her novels portray the subjective world that exists alongside the worlds of the everyday and the material. But other male members of the Group also took their stand against what they saw as the conventional expectations of masculinity, and particularly the expectations that upper-middle-class young men should command others and turn their backs on the worlds of the imagination and the aesthetic. In this sense the Group did no more than other rich young men had done for centuries: the poets Shelley and Byron had rebelled against the expectations of their class and forged for themselves worlds committed to the vindication of sensation and feeling. But the Bloomsbury Group forged their resistance to masculinity at a time when the masculine, and the appearance of the masculine, played a significant part in the making and the keeping of the Empire and the idea of the nation. One of the most famous collective enterprises of the Bloomsbury Group was the Dreadnought Hoax of 1910: an exercise in complex disguise in which members of the Group, covered in black face dye and dressed in flowing robes, presented themselves as members of an Abyssinian delegation to review the battleship *Dreadnought*. The disguise was completely successful; the friends were received with respect and received on board the *Dreadnought* with due deference. The hoax combined 'all possible forms of subversion: ridicule of empire, infiltration of the nation's defences, mockery of bureaucratic procedures, cross-dressing and sexual ambiguity'.[1] The hoax achieved exactly what its participants wanted: it made a mockery of the more pompous aspects of a social hierarchy and made ridiculous the men who ran it.

But another reading of the Dreadnought Hoax is that what it involved was a group of upper-class people, with radical views, playing games on a similar group, with rather more conventional ideas. The exercise of disguise involved the parody of an African language (so much so that Abyssinians became, in popular mythology forever associated with a language described as Bunga-Bunga) and arguably rather more disrespect to the Abyssinians on the part of the deceivers than the deceived. However we read the episode, it was part of those 'culture wars' in Britain in the years just before the outbreak of the First World War; the clashes in the Dreadnought Hoax were not themselves serious, but what underlay them was entirely so. Woolf recognized the relevance and the seriousness of these contests; she wrote, for example in 1908: '*The Daily Telegraph* is discussing the sanctity of marriage and all the deserted wives and husbands in the country are wondering how far the marriage service represents the true word of God. Such a display of imbecility is hardly credible.'[2]

Woolf, in these debates, was quite clearly on the side of what was to become identified with the 'modern', a toleration of sexual ambiguity (indeed a dislike of aggressive sexual certainty), an openness to ideas and influences from other societies and a rejection of automatic loyalty to nation, Established Church and the monarchy. On the other side in this debate were those who regarded any departure from the norms of unquestioning patriotism and acceptance of all forms of traditional authority as something close to treachery. Woolf's concerns, and those of some other members of the Group, for example the painter Duncan Grant and the critic Roger Fry, were essentially with the aesthetic of the modern; their battles were fought with the pen and on canvas. Although Woolf showed, in her letters and diaries (as much as in *A Room of One's Own*) a very realistic grasp of the centrality of money (or lack of it) to the nature of human experience, she seldom took part in public political activism.

These questions – the questions of state and society and the relation of state to state – were the questions which were explored by Virginia's husband Leonard and by their mutual friend Keynes. Leonard Woolf, prior to his marriage to Virginia, had served as a civil administrator in what was then Ceylon. This had given him much the same sense of the ambiguities of Empire and colonialism as it had another, rather younger, servant of the Empire, George Orwell. Both men had resigned from their jobs because they could no longer tolerate the structure of authority of which they were part. Both recognized (Woolf rather more than Orwell) that the Empire could not be maintained for ever, but both also thought that the values brought by the British to their colonial possessions were not all negative. In this, Woolf was entirely a modernist in that he took the view – implicitly rather than explicitly – that there were such things as 'progress' and 'emancipation' and that some aspects of British colonial administration could, for example, give to the colonies rather more just and even humane ways of settling disputes than had formally been the case. The state, in this case, the British state, was not necessarily bad, nor was its intervention in human affairs always to be derided. Indeed, this view was shared by Keynes, by far the most publicly influential member of the Bloomsbury Group and a man whose advocacy of state investment in the economy was to underpin the economic policies of most western societies until challenged by the conservatism of the 1970s.

In both their social and their political views the Bloomsbury Group sat firmly on the side of the modern in the divide which was part of British culture in the years before the First World War. The historian George Dangerfield characterized this division as 'the strange death of liberal England' (in his book of the same name, published in 1935), and although we would probably see nothing 'strange' today about the disappearance of the conventional views of the period just before 1914, Dangerfield's book gives some sense of the possibilities of change both recognized and resisted in those years. In 1914, however, the cultural politics of militarism and nationalism took a sharp turn towards the real: culture stopped being a matter of different views and became a matter of war, and a war which was to determine much of the course of the twentieth century. E.J. Hobsbawm has written of the outbreak of war:

> Like a thunderstorm it broke the heavy closeness of expectation and cleared the air. It meant an end to the superficialities and frivolities of bourgeois society, the boring gradualism of nineteenth century improvement, the tranquillity and peaceful order which was the liberal utopia for the twentieth century and which Nietzsche had prophetically denounced, together with 'the pallid hypocrisy administered by mandarins'.[3]

Nietzsche's prophetic comment on the cultural origins of the First World War is hugely suggestive about the impact of nineteenth-century theories of social progress on the social psyche, since it allows us to consider both the First World War and the rise of European fascism not just in terms of the treaty alliances throughout Europe in 1914 or the economic ruin of Weimar Germany, but also in terms of the interpretation that individuals put on these events and their consequences. Material explanations of the First World War point to the various forms of competition, be they colonial, commercial and naval between European powers prior to 1914, to the 'blank cheque' condoning military action which Germany sent to Austria-Hungary in July 1914, and to the system of almost secret diplomacy which made impossible effective diplomacy. All these are important and valid reasons why war occurred at the time that it did. But equally important is consideration of the socio-psychological argument which sees the outbreak of war as in some sense a social and cultural need to endorse, and make real, those values of militarism and patriotism of which subversives and radicals had been so critical. In support of this argument one factor is perhaps critically important: the huge popular enthusiasm for the war throughout Europe, an enthusiasm which could be found across all class lines. Max Weber was amongst those who welcomed the war as a way of solving the rivalries of Europe, and the Austrian philosopher Wittgenstein went off to war without recorded dissent. Thus, in August 1914, Britain, France and Russia declared war on Germany and Austria-Hungary.

That enthusiasm – an enthusiasm which had been built on the assumption that 'the War will be over by Christmas' – did not last for the duration of the war. Almost immediately, the losses and the brutality of the fighting were horrific. Paul Fussell, in *The Great War in Modern Memory*, offers an instance of the rapid impact of the war: on 11 October 1914 the British army reduced the height requirement for volunteers from five feet eight inches (in August 1914) to five feet five inches. Losses mounted on all sides as the list of the pointless battles went on: the Somme, Ypres, Passchendaele. Britain lost a total of 370,000 men in the fighting, and by the end of the war half of the British army was under the age of 19. But Britain and France did emerge from the war with an intact state, unlike Germany, Russia and Austria-Hungary all of whom lost their monarchs, and their previous form of government, in more, or less, revolutionary ways. The incompetence of the Russian military commanders contributed to the success of the Russian Revolution of 1917, and the war left Germany not just defeated but also in political chaos and confusion.

The people who met to decide the future of Germany and Austria-Hungary did so in Versailles in 1919. Essentially France, Britain and the United States (which had entered in war in 1917) were there to dictate peace terms to the Germans and to redistribute some of the territory which had once belonged to both the Germans and the Austro-Hungarians. Amongst the participants around the conference table was Maynard Keynes, representing the British Treasury, but eventually so disgusted by both the participants and the conclusions of the talks that he resigned and published his *The Economic Consequences of the Peace*. What Keynes argued in this immediately successful book was twofold: the people making the treaty were the prisoners of their own prejudices and cultures, and the conclusions they reached would impoverish not just Germany but the whole of Europe. In his critical accounts of the French prime minister Clemenceau and the president of the United States Woodrow Wilson, Keynes gives a picture of leaders unable to understand anything beyond their own experience, men whose knowledge of the world is so proscribed that they cannot imagine other possibilities than the conventional. Keynes described Woodrow Wilson as a 'blind and deaf Don Quixote' and a man whose 'slowness amongst the Europeans was noteworthy'.[4] The vast new wealth of the United States had not created equally vast comprehension; on the contrary, the country was materially wealthy but conceptually poor.

Keynes was to return to official positions within the British government in the next great war of the twentieth century, between 1939 and 1945. But what he had identified, in his snapshot portraits of the men at the Versailles conference table, was a sense of people as made by cultures, of the difficulty of ensuring that the most critical decisions that affect huge numbers of people are not made by those whose horizons are those of conformity to social norms and conventions. Across Europe at the same time as the deliberations were taking place at Versailles, sociologists, writers and critics were also pondering the nature of the modern world and doing so within those new frameworks which had been shattered by 1914. By that time, Freud had written some of his greatest work, Picasso had exhibited and, in the arts generally, there was a general sense of the possibilities inherent in a radical rupture with the past. The First World War itself created a whole new generation of poets and writers (amongst them Robert Graves, Isaac Rosenberg, Siegfried Sassoon and Wilfred Owen), but in many ways just as important as these impassioned responses to the horrific reality of war were writers such as the German sociologist George Simmel (1858–1918) and the Hungarian literary critic Georg Lukács (1885–1971). The poetry of the First World War is deservedly known for its vivid evocation of the horror of the trenches and the indifference to slaughter and death on the part of those in authority. But this response, vital and lasting as it was, was not in itself innovative: it was a passionate outcry against human suffering, in a tradition which had occurred before and tragically was to occur again. What writers such as Simmel and Lukács did (and in fiction the Irish novelist James Joyce (1882–1941), the Frenchman Marcel Proust (1871–1992) and the American Sinclair Lewis (1885–1951)) was to identify, and in various ways (fictional or otherwise) try to analyse the particular features of what they saw as the 'new' world of the twentieth century. These writers, in different ways and in different contexts, recognized that the form of society in which they lived – that of industrial capitalism – was qualitatively different from previous forms of society. In his writing, Marx had written of the 'alienation' of the worker in capitalism and it was this theme which was to be explored and developed by the French sociologist Emile Durkheim and his contemporary Simmel.

Of all the writers whose work was appearing in the first two decades of the twentieth century it was perhaps Simmel, more than any other, who defined what many other authors and writers were to see as the definitive characteristic of the twentieth century: the solitude at the heart of modern capitalism. The domination of all human relationships by money, and calculations about money, what Marx had described as the 'cash nexus', had the result of making human life a solitary, and indeed solipsistic enterprise. In the various intellectual circles of Europe, in Budapest, Paris, Vienna and Berlin, these ideas and their implications were part and parcel of the life of the avant-garde. In Britain, where the impact of the First World War had been more focused on the loss of life and ways of preventing the repetition of such a catastrophe, the impact of these ideas was less immediate, in part because intellectual life in Britain had not been as receptive as Continental Europe to the new discipline of sociology. But Virginia Woolf certainly recognized the centrality of money (and lack of it) to human experience, and the poet T.S. Eliot (an American who spent much of his adult life in Britain) wrote, in *The Waste Land* (published in 1922), of what he saw as the collapse of civilized values and the bleakness of contemporary life. In his later work, for example *Notes Towards a Definition of Culture*, which was published in 1948, Eliot was to enlarge on his theme of what he saw as the destruction of 'high' culture by the commercial and marketplace pressures of the modern world. But by that time, of course, the 'culture wars' of the twentieth century had taken another devastating toll on human life.

What can be seen emerging in Europe in the years after the end of the First World War is an increasingly self-confident sense of the modern (in science, the arts, and architecture and design) together with – and usually associated with it – the assumption that 'modern' understanding did not involve the kind of mass, licensed violence that had been unleashed in the First World War. 'Modern' people (the people who set up the League of Nations and contributed in their millions to initiatives for world peace and understanding) did not need wars to solve their difficulties and, theoretically, at least, were aware of how to plan cities, improve diet, curtail physical suffering and order the urban world in rational ways. The improvements in medical science of the nineteenth century had been much enhanced by the hideous needs of war: for plastic surgery, for psychological understanding of trauma, for blood transfusion and perhaps not least, for the prevention of the spread of sexually transmitted disease. The British army took it upon itself to lecture its soldiers on the use of the rubber contraceptive: a lesson of war which was not to be lost in peacetime. The soldiers who returned home to Britain in 1918 (ostensibly to a 'land fit for heroes' which was actually nothing of the kind) took with them in this latter case a valuable lesson for civilian life and a lesson which was to play a significant part in the fall of the British population in the 1920s and 1930s. The soldiers returned to the usual patriotic outpourings but also to a world in which certain features of modern urban experience had now become commonplace: advertising, mass entertainment and the idea, if not the reality, of the 'emancipation' of women. War, as historians often remind us, had once again been the engine of social change: in Britain one of its most marked effects was to decrease radically the number of domestic servants. The need for extra workers in both manufacturing and service industries was met by the employment of women: single working-class women who in the pre-war years had often had little alternative except to work in the household of the better-off could now work in the relative personal freedom of the labour market.

The world of the years immediately after the First World War were years, for much of Europe and many Europeans, of reconstruction and relative peace. Germany established democratic government, Britain voted into power its first Labour government, and France and Italy took steps towards a degree of industrialization. In Britain it was the domestic relations of class politics, rather than those with foreign powers, which interrupted this civil peace. In 1926, British trade unions attempted to compel the government to make some concessions towards the terrible poverty of their members: the then privately owned mines and railways stood firmly with the government whilst for a week the country took sides in the General Strike. What emerged from this – apart from even more hardship for mining communities – was a loss of trade union confidence which was not to return until the years of the Second World War. The 'ruling' class, the bourgeoisie, the wealthy, the powerful, had won a lasting victory over organized labour that was to set the class lines of Britain for a generation. For some social groups in Britain the 1920s and the 1930s were times of material improvement: this was the era of the beginning of private car ownership, of the construction of swathes of suburbs around many cities with houses inexpensive enough for purchase and a degree of mechanization of the home. But against this gradual improvement could be set the continued poverty of areas of heavy industry: the north-east and north-west of Britain and the Welsh mining communities. These places – as Orwell was to describe in *The Road to Wigan Pier* – shared none of the limited prosperity of other parts of the country, and government welfare policies, such as the hated means test, inflicted humiliation on the recipients.

The decline in the prosperity of manufacturing areas in England and Scotland was in part due to the economic competition which Britain, and other European powers, were facing from what was becoming the world's most powerful economy – that of the United States. The United States was the first country in the world to adopt the system of production known as scientific management, or Taylorism, after its author, F.W. Taylor. Taylor had likened the human body to a machine and conducted time and motion studies to determine the most efficient way to make use of it. Taylorism was then related to mass production and in particular the factory-based assembly lines of the car manufacturer Henry Ford. What came to be known as Fordism was a way of producing goods which separated workers from one another and gave to each group of workers control and involvement in only a small part of the production process. In the Ford factories of Detroit and in factories throughout the United States, workers began to produce goods – particularly what became known as consumer goods – with amazing speed and efficiency. Few factories in Europe could match this productivity, nor could most of Europe provide the huge internal economic markets which underpinned the success of American domestic production. Yet this picture of the United States as a hugely successful economic power has to be heavily qualified by the problems of overproduction and lack of capital which resulted in the Wall Street Crash of 1929 – a dramatic fall in the value of privately owned stocks and shares which was to send the American economy, and the economies of Europe, into recession.

The Wall Street Crash of 1929, with its dramatic pictures of suicides and queues of unemployed workers, marks the beginning of the conditions which were to result in the rise of European fascism. By 1929 the economies of Europe and the United States were closely involved: a fall in the value of the dollar was as disastrous for Europe as it was for the United States. In Germany the Deutschmark lost its value, galloping inflation swept away the value of savings, and investments became worthless overnight. What had looked, in Germany and other parts of Europe, like post-war recovery and the beginnings of prosperity started to look like a plunge into wholesale poverty and uncertainty. Yet the crisis, although dramatic, was relatively short-lived and, largely because of the influence of Keynesian economics, the economy of the United States started to recover. Government spending slowly began to restore confidence and a degree of stability seemed to return to world markets.

Nevertheless, an economic system had been plunged into chaos and what Europe and the United States had seen was the possibility of the collapse of an economic system and the social system with which it was intertwined. Capitalism (which Marx had predicted would always be accompanied by crises) now demonstrably looked like an insecure and unreliable way of organizing the world; just when Europeans had grown used to the idea of managing nature in ways that guaranteed sufficiency, so another uncertainty appeared in the world. But this new uncertainty – unlike that of nature – was not accompanied by a recognition that little could be done to ensure its reliability. By 1929 there were many in Europe who argued that capitalism was by its very nature an insecure and unreliable economic system, subject to all kinds of crises. The only way to secure material sufficiency for all, and an absence of the kinds of crises which seemed to be an inevitable part of capitalism, was through socialism and planned economies. The 'free' market, its critics suggested, was always going to be one which inflicted endless hardship on the most vulnerable and could not guarantee the continuation of the kinds of state benefits which by the beginning of the 1930s had come to be expected in a number of – although not all – European states.

Socialism, in the form of state socialism, had arrived in Russia in 1917, and although its early years had been marked by famines worse than any previously endured, the country had, by 1930, initiated a series of plans to direct the economy. The world could now see a planned, centralized economy in which the state made the decisions about the economy and made those decisions, at least nominally, in the light of the interests of all its citizens. For many in Europe in the

1920s and early 1930s, Russia represented hope for the future, a way of running industrial societies which did not penalize the poor and the powerless. Communism and socialism were the possibilities against which capitalist democracies were placed; what was appealing was the idea that the social world could be organized and run predictably. For many people who had no particular ideological enthusiasm for communism or socialism the idea of planning was the central and important idea. It was, too, an idea which fitted in with many of the values of modernism: the idea of a house as a 'machine for living in', the training of the body in order to ensure fitness, and the use of machines for domestic work all suggested, albeit implicitly, the view that the world, and one's part in it, need not be a haphazard or accidental affair but one which is decided rationally and then organized accordingly.

The various threads of modernism in art, architecture and fiction were thus interwoven with ideas about the rational organization of society and the planned organization of the body. For example, it is in the 1920s and 1930s that the ideas of 'planned' parenthood and the 'planning' of care for babies and infants become visible. Many of these ideas were seized upon with enthusiasm by sections of the population, but at the same time the idea of 'planning', and more particularly of socialist planning, was regarded with deep disfavour, not to say outright hostility, by those who had the most to lose from public ownership. Within the many strands of thought that confront us by the beginning of the 1930s there was both enthusiasm for the modern and concern about its politics, since from its inception modernism (be it the work of Freud or Picasso or Woolf or the Bauhaus) had been associated with the socially progressive and a challenge to traditional certainties, notably about nation and gender. Modernism was, from its outset, transcultural and transnational: it recognized (often obliquely) that industrial capitalism was a world system and that the way of life which it created would be similar whatever the national context. As was to become clear in the years after the Second World War, industrial capitalism could eradicate many differences of culture and nationality. But, at the same time, industrial capitalism brought with it the domination of man by machine, the erosion of the local, and the 'iron cage' (in Weber's terminology) of bureaucratic organization.

The sense of loss of control of both the nation and the culture was very much part of the rise of fascism in Europe. The reasons for the rise to power of Hitler in Germany, Mussolini in Italy and Franco in Spain have different particular reasons and different cultural roots. What we can note is that of the three European fascist leaders only Franco in Spain came to power (and stayed in power) with an agenda which gave any kind of prominence to religious ideas. Indeed, what is striking about the politics of Europe after the First World War is how secular they became: the Christian God had played a part (albeit not a very significant one) in British propaganda about the war of 1914–18, but by 1933 and the coming to power of Hitler in Germany the issues at stake were secular issues. Society had become, by this time, not just 'modern' but also secular. But for many people the new kind of society which had emerged in Europe since the end of the First World War was intensely problematic: the modern was clearly deeply attractive, yet at the same time it seemed to break down barriers and hierarchies which people had taken for granted for generations. The implicit sense of the possibility of control over the world, and oneself, that the modern contained seemed to leave little space for spontaneity, the great cultural symbols of the nation and differentiated masculinity and femininity. If machines were going to take over the physical work of the world, and the public world encourage the participation of women in it, what space was left in this modern metropolis for the male? It was a question which the culture of the 1930s answered in different ways: Hollywood cinema reinvented the heroic male in the genre of westerns and one of the most popular films of the time (*King Kong*) saw the city threatened by an alliance of woman and beast: the revenge of Nature. The Auden generation of poets in Britain defined what Christopher Caudwell called a 'dying culture' and distanced themselves from all traditional forms of behaviour and authority. The future seemed to be both planned and androgynous.

It was this culture that fascism challenged, in its veneration of the idea of masculine physical strength, a strength only to be found in certain racial groups and the male sex. The nation, and the idea of the nation, became a new organizing symbol. It was no longer the creaking and incompetent structure of the past but a new and efficient organization which could, through centrist economic planning, produce goods, secure employment and reliable services. An aspect of the modern which had originally been part of left wing and radical politics became part of the right. In this, fascism accorded with, rather than rejected, the modern. But where it did not accord with the modern, and where its cultural values were made most transparent, was in the politics of gender and the arts. Fascism reasserted the fantasy of the authority of men and the patriarchal order of the nuclear family. (Both these social forms had existed as fact in Europe, but any history of the family from the eighteenth century onwards will also point to the diverse forms of families and the considerable, and powerful, part played by women within them.) Nor was the reassertion just at the level of fantasy: Nazi Germany barred married women from much paid work and many of the professions; even at the height of its need for extra labour power, women were not conscripted until January 1943, and then with many exceptions.[5] Those methods of birth control which were gradually becoming more common in northern Europe – contraception and, for the rich, abortion – were outlawed. The prevailing ideal of the family became one which for much of the population had never been anything except a fantasy: a powerful and employed male providing for a wife and children.

Just as fascism reinvented traditional gender norms, so it reinvented the nation. The glorification of the days of power of the nation became part and parcel of fascist regimes: for Mussolini the great days of the Roman Empire and for Hitler the creation of a mythical, all-powerful Germany, whose racial qualities alone in Europe could keep away Bolshevism, Judaism and modernism. The nation – in Germany, Spain and Italy – now took on the role of the cultural bastion against the modern: the 'depraved' modern art, the critical literature, the sceptical social sciences and anything that seemed to be tainted with ideas of gender ambiguity were labelled dangerous and suspect. Throughout Europe there was clearly a degree of sympathy for these ideas in those countries which did not vote into power fascist dictators. Britain, in the 1930s, embraced the mock Tudor in architecture with much more enthusiasm than it did modern architecture, women writers of detective fiction valorized the England of country houses and largely condemned – except in the old, in the case of Miss Marple – the idea of female agency. Nevertheless the culture was moving towards that recognizably modern self in which the right to personal happiness is central and of far greater importance than any other allegiance. When Edward VIII of England abdicated in order to marry Wallis Simpson he spoke of his decision in terms of individual fulfilment, the right to be with the 'woman I love'. He did not speak of religious issues about the question of divorce (as Princess Margaret was to do in the 1950s) but what he did assert was his right to be happy. Many of his subjects wished him well, not just out of human sympathy but because Britain by

1936 had seen the arrival of values which emphasized the right to individuals of happiness, be it through personal relationships or engagement with what was merging as a consumer society.

The Second World War of 1939–45 brutally interrupted this culture and the way of life of much of Europe. The war brought devastation and tragedy to millions; occupation, forced migration and the persecution of the Jews involved civilians in the war quite as much as members of the armed forces. The Soviet Union lost more soldiers than any other European power, yet it was the defeat of Hitler's armies by the Russians at Stalingrad that marked the military turning point of the war. The entry of the United States into the war after the Japanese bombed the naval port of Pearl Harbour in 1941 ensured that the resources of the United States (of manpower, equipment and raw materials) would be available, and for a very short period, Britain, the United States and the Soviet Union fought as allies. When peace eventually came, in 1945, Britain, like parts of the Netherlands, Germany and France, was bombed and bankrupt; the immediate priorities of the post-war years were to be reconstruction and ensuring that the end of this war offered something better to both soldiers and civilians than the end of the First World War had done. The Labour government of 1945–50 received a huge popular mandate for the implementation of social policies that would provide an effective welfare state. By 1950 this had been largely achieved and the recommendations of the Liberal peer Lord Beveridge, that the state should provide assistance for its citizens 'from cradle to grave', had been put into place.

Much of the groundwork for the coming of the welfare state to Britain had been put into place during the war, when the state took over control of aspects of production, employment and consumption. In the conscription of unmarried and childless women, the rationing of food and consumer goods, and restrictions on travel, the state had a considerable impact on the lives of its citizens, an impact which it furthered by extensive propaganda on all aspects of social life. It was this extension of state intervention in the private sphere which produced part of the inspiration for George Orwell's *1984*. Published in 1949 this novel was to provide an account of the modern world (and a vocabulary for it) which was to inform later ideas about the modern state and the lives of citizens. *1984* is, however, just one reading of the world after 1945: a reading which emphasizes not just state control but also the disappearance of history, civil liberties and a private space. It is a reading which is deeply pessimistic about the future of democracy and liberty. Other accounts of the impact of the Second World War echo aspects of Orwell's account: for example, the historian Paul Addison has argued that what emerged during the Second World War was a consensus of belief in state planning and social engineering. The view of the 'post-war consensus' (and a consensus during the war itself) had its critics, but what did become accepted, until it was challenged by Margaret Thatcher in 1979, was the view that it was the responsibility of the state to ensure social justice and material provision.

In the decades after the Second World War Britain, and British society, were to undergo a number of major transformations. In the years after 1945, Britain lost much of its overseas empire and its status as a world power was much diminished. During the Cold War, which ended the co-operation between the Soviet Union and the United States during the war, Britain took the side of the United States and was to remain firmly within those political boundaries for the rest of the twentieth century. But the lives of British citizens in the period between 1945 and 2000 were to be transformed less by these global politics than by other seismic changes in the everyday world. Amongst these changes it is possible to define two which perhaps had the most impact on the lives of ordinary citizens and which then produced a huge theoretical literature of explanation and in some cases justification. These notable changes were the trans-formation of industry, from a manufacturing to a service economy, the emergence of the citizen as a 'consumer', and the social and sexual revolutions of the 1960s. Against these changes can be set the persistence in Britain of inequalities of class and the ownership of wealth: the country changed hugely in terms of much of its everyday behaviour but the structural divisions of class remained remarkably intact.

The manufacturing industries of Britain had been, in many cases, the leaders of the Industrial Revolution of the nineteenth century. The emergence of other European countries as significant industrial powers, and even more critically the emergence of the United States, had challenged and eventually undermined this position. Britain, by the end of the 1950s, simply could not compete in terms of the production of manufactured goods, particularly consumer goods, with other countries. It began to become clear that Britain needed to develop a new technological and scientific com-petence if it was to take part in what the Labour prime minister Harold Wilson once described as the 'white hot heat of the technological revolution'. Unfortunately for Britain, the white hot heat seemed to suit other countries rather better than it did Britain and the decline of manufacturing industry continued. Governments throughout the 1960s and the 1970s continued to support sections of British industry (for example car manufacturing), but by the late 1970s a new economic theory had come to challenge this orthodoxy of state support: Milton Friedmann and the Chicago School of economists had made their mark. The Conservative Party, led by Margaret Thatcher, came to power in 1979 on a mandate of reducing the role and the responsibilities of the state, and, in 1980, with similar policies, Ronald Reagan was elected president of the United States. The acceptance of Keynes and neo-Keynesian economics had been challenged.

But if the impact of the work of one member of the Bloomsbury Group was beginning to decline, some of the other aspects of their ideas were gradually becoming part of everyday existence. Blooms- bury had been tolerant of homosexuality, of relationships outside the formal bonds of marriage and had resolutely opposed the form- ality of social life. The Group was by no means the first group of people to live outside conventional society, but even they had had to compromise some of their views. By 1980 this would no longer have been necessary: a toleration of open homosexuality (and certainly its decriminalization) had begun, 'living together', outside conven- tional marriage had become largely unremarkable and the very concept of illegitimacy had acquired the ring of the past. As the sociologist Elizabeth Wilson was to put it: 'We are all bohemians now'.[6] These changes did not, however, go uncontested. For sections of the population the 'sexual revolution' of the 1960s and the 1970s was a step towards social decay, and legislation which changed the laws on divorce, abortion and homosexuality was bitterly fought. But opposition to changing social mores could not stop that change: the full employment of the post-war years had given people confidence in the opportunities rather than the constraints of the social world, a confidence which government policies such as the expansion of higher education were to underpin. Consumer goods (cars, house- hold machinery), which were available before the Second World War to only a small section of the population, became widely available, whilst car ownership transformed the urban landscape. The demo- cratization of travel, the ownership of consumer goods and a widely available popular culture changed the nature of general social experience.

When Virginia Woolf wrote of the nature of urban experience in her novels and essays of the 1920s and 1930s she was writing of the early years of modernism. When she committed suicide in 1940 she did so at a point where it was apparent that modernism could produce conflict as much as it could produce understanding. The fascist powers of Europe came to power for numerous reasons, but part of the psychic energy which fascism drew upon was a furious resistance to everything that modernism stood for: democracy, cultural diversity and tolerance and the rational and secular ordering of the social world. One of the most tragic paradoxes of the twentieth century is that fascism itself was to draw on one of the traditions of modernism: the ability to plan and order the social world. The German assault on the Jews (the 'final solution') was constructed within the parameters of the Enlightenment paradigm of problem and resolution. The very Enlightenment exercise of diminishing religious authority and putting in its place the centrality of the social and what is constructed through human agency allowed politics and political decisions to take place outside the boundaries of moral debate. It was this moral absence at the heart of the modern which Orwell recognized, and explored in *1984*: the society which becomes its own justification, because it has eliminated all other values. It is this construct of society, which does not question the form or the nature of 'society' which has become part of the western paradigm. Since the fall of the Berlin wall in 1989 it is increasingly a paradigm which involves no defence; without the existence of socialism there is no necessary legitimation of the market economy.

The form of society in which we live in Britain at the beginning of the twenty-first century is thus a society which sees little need to explain or justify itself. Although structural inequalities of class persist throughout the West, the lives of many citizens are vastly more comfortable than they were in 1900. Life expectancy is greater, education is more widely available, the plurality of social norms allows more individual freedom, and private and public work is no longer as physically demanding as in the past. At this point it is often the case that the negative side of the equation is put: the supposed breakdown in family life, the erosion of secure boundaries of personal and social behaviour and the greater personal stress involved in every aspect of private life, from the policing of the body to demanding degrees of self-consciousness about formerly unselfconscious aspects of existence. But much of this exercise demands certainty about the past: about a belief in those assertions of previous periods of stability and self-confidence. On this the historical record would suggest that there has been no shift from past certainty to present insecurity; degrees of risk, for example, are no greater in 2000 than they were in 1900. But what modernism has given us is lived experience of a secular and a democratic world: for the first time in human history religion and religious belief became optional, just as democracy has provided us with a model (albeit often imperfect in practice) of equality, not just of recognition, but also of agency, between human beings.

Chapter 5

What Happened in History

1821   Publication of Saint-Simon's *Industrial System*
1824   Publication of Auguste Comte's *System of Positive Politics*
1846   Publication of Marx and Engels' *The German Ideology*
1895   Publication of Emile Durkheim's *The Division of Labour in Society*
1897   Publication of Durkheim's *Suicide*
1900   Publication of Georg Simmel's *The Philosophy of Money*
1904/5 Publication of Max Weber's *The Protestant Ethic and the Spirit of Capitalism*
1912   Publication of Durkheim's *The Elementary Forms of the Religious Life*
1922   Publication (posthumously) of Weber's *Economy and Society*
1972   Publication of Michel Foucault's *The Archeology of Knowledge*
1972   Publication of Sheila Rowbotham's *Hidden from History*
1976   Publication of Juliet Mitchell's *Psychoanalysis and Feminism*

The period from 1500 to 2000 is, for most of us, a period which we can only regard with profound awe (and sometimes despair) at the changes which have taken place. We generally assume that a time traveller arriving in the Europe of 2000 from the Europe of 1500 would be amazed and bewildered by this new world. But if we consider some of the continuities between 1500 and 2000 this conclusion might be less automatic. Amongst the continuities that stretch across the centuries is, for the British, the nation and the monarchy. Although union of the English and Scottish crowns did not take place until 1603 (and that union was still to be contested), the throne of England has continued (with a brief interregnum) across the centuries. The power of the monarch has been much diminished, but it still stands as an emblem (and a not altogether redundant one) of a social and political hierarchy. If we move just a few decades into the sixteenth century we come across another striking parallel between 1500 and 2000, in that the British monarch is still the head of the established Church. Church and state remain linked in Britain in ways which were as true for the sixteenth century as they are today. Despite the widespread view that we now live in a secular society, the British state itself is indissolubly linked to a particular religion. Our citizen of 1500, surveying 2000, might be amazed at the industrial, urban world which has been created, but national loyalty would still be linked to loyalty to the Christian, Anglican Church. If the time travellers looked away from the new cities and towns born of industrialization they might also find that aspects of the ownership of land have not changed as much as might be expected: large landowners still own vast areas of the countryside and the urban world. Even though the social power of the aristocracy might have ended in the nineteenth century, as David Cannadine has suggested, certain once-wealthy families are still wealthy families in the twenty-first century.[1] For example, the Spencer family – made famous through the marriage of Diana Spencer to Prince Charles – made a fortune in sheep farming in the sixteenth century and has managed to retain considerable wealth. It may well be that the aristocracy 'declined' in the sense of losing estates and political power but they did not lose the power to fascinate and to act as an aspirational model for certain sections of society. The late Tory MP and diarist Alan Clark, although a member of a family which made its money through trade (Clark's cotton thread), persistently paraded himself as an 'aristocrat' and a member of the 'upper classes'.

So the social revolution which is sometimes taken for granted between 1500, or any other date between the sixteenth century and the present day, has to be regarded with some suspicion. The great 'isms' of modern society and importantly the grand themes of modern sociology are industrialization, urbanization, secularization, rationalization, individualization and state formation: all these are aspects of the 'modern', which can only be found in their infancy in the sixteenth century. But – as Derek Sayer points out in *Capitalism and Modernity* – by the sixteenth century free labour and the marketplace had met and the meeting had not escaped the notice of Karl Marx, writing three hundred years later. Sayer writes of Marx's comments: 'In the meeting in the market-place of the free labourer and the capitalist, asserts *Capital*, is comprised "a world's history". Indeed, claims *The German Ideology*, it is capitalism which produced world history for the first time'.[2]

This comment on the sixteenth century provides a salutary

reminder that we live in a world in which the nature of production may have changed dramatically but in which many of the social relations of production have changed rather less than we might like to think. We can recognize that in the west the relations of production have become less immediately brutal than they once were but the concentration of the ownership of wealth has continued to be organized on a pattern of a few owning a great deal and the majority owning rather less. Welfare states and two centuries of organized labour have mitigated the worst extremes of capitalism but social inequality is still part of the social fabric of the west and cannot be assumed to have disappeared with other cultural and social changes that have taken place. It is here that we come to the more dramatic differences between 1500 and 2000, the differences between the way in which we lived then and the way in which we live now. Of the many differences are the facts that we live almost twice as long as our ancestors, women do not routinely die in childbirth, the great majority of children survive beyond the age of four years, and almost all people in the west are both literate and have had some education up to the age of 16. Nature does not expose us to the same perils as in 1500: plague and famine have disappeared from the west, although pessimists might point out that the elimination of the great plagues of the past has been replaced by new diseases such as AIDS. Again, on what would probably be counted on the positive side of human history in the past five hundred years, we no longer burn witches, or generally believe in them, even though our capacity for demonization does not seem to have abated significantly. On those (fortunately few) occasions when tragic crimes are committed, for example the murder of the young child James Bulger, there is still voiced (in the absence of what seems to be an adequate explanation for the crime) a belief in evil. The Roman Catholic Church has abolished hell and purgatory (which would probably have been good news for many citizens in 1500) but what clearly lingers on in the public mind is a realm of the incomprehensible, a world which is no longer about witches and the supernatural but is beyond what is perceived as human understanding.

The event which should have enabled us to leave behind the idea of the incomprehensible – and substituted for it the view that everything that occurs in human society can be explained – is the European Enlightenment of the seventeenth and eighteenth centuries. As we have seen, this event has no defining dates but a number of important landmarks and is generally accepted as a period of transformation in the way in which Europeans came to think about the world. The Enlightenment is, for many writers, always associated with the 'modern', in that the ideas which were part and parcel of the Enlightenment (essentially Kant's 'dare to know') are associated with the coming of science and 'reason'. The problem with this view is twofold: one is that certain sciences (notably mathematics) long pre-dated the Enlightenment and the other is that according to a number of writers, of whom the best-known is the sociologist Zygmunt Bauman, what the Enlightenment brought into being was a construct of reason which was void of moral understanding.[3] Decades before Bauman voiced this view (largely as an explanation of Hitler's assault on the Jews in the period 1933–45) other writers had been equally sceptical about the value of reason and the modern world. The German philosopher Friedrich Nietzsche, writing in the latter part of the nineteenth century, came to the conclusion that 'modern' culture is both decadent and driven by material values. He wrote of a modern world in which 'haste and hurry are now universal' and in which

> The waters of religion are ebbing away and leaving behind swamps or stagnant pools; the nations are again drawing away from one another in the most hostile fashion and long to tear one another to pieces. The sciences, pursued without any restraint and in a spirit of the blindest laissez-faire, are shattering and dissolving all firmly held belief; the educated classes and states are being swept along by a hugely con-temptible money economy. The world has never been more worldly, never poorer in love and goodness. ... Everything, contemporary art and science included, serves the coming barbarism. The cultured man has degenerated to the greatest enemy of culture, for he wants lyingly to deny the existence of the universal sickness and thus obstruct the physicians.[4]

This view of the modern world found its echoes in Britain in the reactions of John Ruskin, William Morris and others to what they saw as the shoddy and the ephemeral nature of the products of a machine age. But Nietzsche's arguments go much further than that of aesthetic horror at the products of the machine age. Nietzsche's view of the modern is not just that of sorrow at the decline of the traditional artisan, it is a rejection of all the assumptions upon which the 'modern' world is built, and in particular the endless pursuit of profit and the absence of anything that might be regarded as transcendent values. Nietzsche, like Marx, is writing of the culture – modernity – which is produced by the modern. For both of them the 'modern' – which is not to be confused with modernity – or indeed modernism – is a period in which the values of the marketplace have replaced all other values. In the context of these arguments, arguments which take on both the culture and the material relations of western society, the Enlightenment is less a time of human understanding and emancipation and more a period of even greater obfuscation of the realities of the social world. The philosophy, and even more so the discipline of sociology which emerged from the Enlightenment, are, then, less radical new ways of studying the world and rather more aspects of that decadent culture itself.

The considerable hostility which Nietzsche expressed towards European society of the nineteenth century is crucial not just because of the relationship of this one author to later developments in European history and philosophy, but also because of the fault lines in post-Enlightenment thought which Nietzsche's work suggests. The Enlightenment allowed, and indeed encouraged, the investigation of the social and the natural world; on that every writer on the Enlightenment would agree. But what went with this, to some observers, was a loss of spontaneity, the irrational, what might generally be described as 'feeling'. If the new model of the human being by the end of the eighteenth century was that of a person who thought about their position in the social world and then constructed it, where did that leave the person who thought rather less and acted with scant reference to the rational. The definitive novelist of the Enlightenment is arguably Jane Austen: in her narratives she suggests that the most admirable way of ordering life is through deliberate thought and the exercise of judgement about it. But Austen herself is well aware of the problems that this deliberate ordering of emotional life might have on human beings: in her novel *Sense and Sensibility* she sets up a division between the heroine who thinks and the heroine who feels. By the end of the novel both these categories have been questioned by Austen but what we have been presented with is precisely that distinction – between thought and feeling, the rational and the irrational – that had come to trouble writers and artists by the end of the eighteenth century. The British Romantic poets, Coleridge (1772–1834), Wordsworth (1770–1850), Byron (1788–1824), Keats (1795–1821) and Shelley (1792–1822) took up, in different ways, the same issue; the concept of the 'ordered life' had come to be intensely problematic since in it there appeared to be little possibility of 'sensation', 'feeling' and those intense relationships rendered irrational by the power of reason.

So what we see by the first decades of the nineteenth century is a questioning less of the value of reason than of the marginalization of the possibilities of the creative and the spontaneous life. It is this fault line which is to become the central tension of European society after the end of the Enlightenment: people recognize that the world can be changed, reconstructed and reordered; life can be lived without God and Nature can be controlled. But the fear starts to emerge, and is to initiate the tradition which extends from the Romantic poets to George Orwell, that too much 'order' in the social world diminishes the possibilities of human existence. In this tradition we can situate many of the social changes and the social movements that make up the history of the nineteenth and the twentieth centuries: the growth of social bohemianism, the cult of the artist as the socially marginal figure, the aesthetization of politics and the fascist admiration for charisma and the extraordinary. As increased production made possible the more democratic possession of goods and tolerable standards of living, so the appeal of the apparently spontaneous increased; order and planning gave western societies prosperity but to many citizens they seemed to remove authenticity of feeling and experience. Within this analysis many writers on the twentieth century have explained momentous social events as the rise of fascism and, less socially destructively, the furious hedonism of youth culture.

It is in explanations of the rise of fascism that we can find many of the different ideas about the history of the past two centuries. The First World War was a war in which military casualties on all sides were appalling and the incompetence of the military high command legendary. But it was the Second World War which truly involved both civilians and soldiers, and was a war in which the loss of life reached extraordinary figures. Equally, the genesis of the Second World War can be explained in part by that fissure in European culture suggested above: a fissure which counterposed order with action and was to be employed by Hitler with dramatically effective results. We have in the rise of fascism both strong material arguments (the collapse of the German economy and widespread poverty and unemployment) with powerful cultural arguments, the emergence of a leader who can articulate a sense of a collective will, a will which can counter the inertia of bureaucracy and ineffective politics.

The appeal of fascism is thus that it can both restore order (in the sense of providing food and employment) and challenge it (in asserting alternative forms of politics to those which seem to promise only stasis). What we reach, in Europe in the 1930s, is a point in history where an evident economic crisis takes a particular direction for reasons that do not emerge from the purely economic. For people living in Germany or the United States or Britain at the time, the promise of the modern world had suddenly been snatched away. The only possibility for the restoration of that modern world seemed, to some, to lie in a return to a fantasy of the past. The association of the modern with democracy was restored in 1945, but events of 1933–45 had shown the capacity of the modern, mechanized, world to a return to a pre-modern past.

The best-known theorists of the rise of fascism, and in particular German fascism, are the group of sociologists known collectively as the Frankfurt School. The great names in this group include Theodor Adorno (1903–69), Herbert Marcuse (1898–1979), Leo Lowenthal (1900–93), Marie Jahoda (1907–2001) and Max Horkheimer (1895–1973). All of them were associated with the Institut für Sozialforschung at the University of Frankfurt, an institution founded by Felix Weil in 1922 but largely dismantled and moved to Columbia University, New York, after Hitler came to power in 1933. This group, sometimes known by the term 'critical theorists', are primarily concerned with the implications of the consequences of the Enlightenment. What they saw was the potentially stifling consequences of excessive bureaucracy and the capacity of modern societies to control their members. For this group of writers, material reality did not determine consciousness; they were not explicitly anti-Marxist but they did take issue with the version of Marxism that was becoming the orthodoxy in the Soviet Union after Stalin came to power. The history of the Frankfurt School is long and complex; their engagements with other writers and members of European intellectual life from the 1920s onwards was considerable. One of the best known of their debates was with the German playwright Bertolt Brecht (1898–1956), whom they viewed as something of a vulgar materialist. But their influence was considerable and what they established was a remarkable tradition of the study of the social world which remains highly influential, not least because it attempts to integrate an analysis of the social with the insights of psychoanalysis.

The lasting heritage of the work of the Frankfurt School was to bequeath to European social theory a way of looking at the social world, which, like Marxism, did not take capitalism as a natural given of the social world. Unlike Marxism, however, the work of the Frankfurt School allowed a considerable space for the cultural; members of the group wrote both on large-scale social events and on literature and music. It was in this context that they came into conflict with both Brecht and with one of the most famous writers on the modern, Walter Benjamin (1892–1940), who was to become widely known for his essay 'The work of art in an age of mechanical reproduction' and for his account of the early years of modern urban life, *The Arcades Project*.[5] Relations between Benjamin and the Frankfurt School were often tense: Horkheimer rejected Benjamin's graduate thesis and in doing so effectively excluded Benjamin from an academic career. But Benjamin's examination of modern capitalism has, like the work of the Frankfurt School, stood the test of time, not least because the subject which is of primary concern to Benjamin – that of the impact of commodity fetishism – shows no sign of abating in the West.

The themes explored by the Frankfurt School and by Benjamin are continued in the work of the German Jurgen Habermas (born in 1929). Again, what is important to Habermas is not so much the capacity of industrial capitalism to produce extraordinary amounts of goods and services as the cultural and social implications of this world. For Habermas, what has happened in the modern world is that knowledge is no longer independent or objective: it has become entangled in the interest of capitalism and instead of serving the interests of objective enquiry it serves the interests of the continuation of a particular form of society. It is not, he suggests, that there is no knowledge in the modern world; on the contrary there is a vast amount of it. But it is not directed towards the enlightenment or the liberation of human beings, except in those tangential ways where there may be a coincidence of the interest of capitalism and the pursuit of knowledge. Of particular concern to Habermas is the problem of the legitimacy of political regimes in industrial capitalism: there is a formal acceptance of democracy, he suggests, throughout much of the west but the working of democracy frequently faces situations where democratic interests conflict with those of the marketplace. These themes are discussed in his most famous works *Legitimation Crisis* (1973) and *The Theory of Communicative Action* (1981). Yet despite what might appear to be pessimism about the world after the Enlightenment, for Habermas its values and its ideas remain worth defending. Unlike some other sociologists he does not abandon or reject the promises of the Enlightenment.

It is, therefore, from Germany, the home of the most powerful fascist regime of European history, that there emerges the most coherent and the most lasting theoretical accounts of what happened in the first part of the twentieth century. In the years before the rise of Hitler the German Weimar Republic had been home to many of the great names of European modernism – the Bauhaus Group, for example, remains synonymous with the development of an instantly recognizable form in architecture and domestic goods. Other European countries had had their own versions of modernist work, but arguably no country had seen, as did Germany, so great a departure from the past and tradition. In much of Europe there emerged a familiarity with the culture, particularly the popular culture, of the United States. The 'great' years of Hollywood translated a new cultural form, the cinema, which had originally emerged in Europe, into a global phenomenon. It was in the years between 1918 and 1939 that mass culture truly emerged, a culture which should be defined in its widest sense to include not just artefacts and a mass media, but also a new way of living in the world, amongst which the characteristic of the absence of social deference is probably the most striking. Hollywood made legends – about the making of the United States, about social mobility and about a more sexualized form of heterosexuality – but it also communicated to its watchers an appetite for the goods and the way of life which it displayed. Goods which were, by this period, becoming available in previously unknown quantities.

Our time traveller would certainly be amazed by the mechanization of the everyday contemporary world, a world in which most people cannot understand the way in which many ordinary, everyday goods are produced. If we citizens of the twenty-first century had to make the goods which make up our daily lives – the cars, the mobile phones, the computers – we would be unable to do so. In the world of the twenty-first century, technical competence has become highly specialist and remote from ordinary understanding. This is not to argue that there was no specialist competence in the sixteenth century, clearly there was and it produced much that was beautiful and lasting. The point is rather that the difference between this specialist competence, be it in architecture or in shipbuilding, was not so far away from skills used in other contexts. Historians of the arts and architecture have pointed to the fact that many of the great buildings of the past were the work not of people whom we would today identify as architects but of particularly talented builders or masons. One of the social changes of the past two hundred years has been the specialization of function in industrial societies, accompanied by the growth of professions and what has sometimes been known as 'professionalization'. The best example of the emergence of a profession is that of medicine. The skill of healing has been recognized for thousands of years; the profession of medicine is rather more recent and dates largely from the eighteenth century and the gradual emergence of specific skills associated with surgery or the treatment of infectious diseases. The barber surgeons of the seventeenth and eighteenth centuries were (rightly) feared members of the community; by the beginning of the twentieth century surgeons had become an elite group within medicine with tightly controlled professional regulation and standards of entry.

The theme of the division of labour in society (and *The Division of Labour in Society* is one of the best known of the works of the French sociologist Emile Durkheim) is one which has, as Durkheim and others would argue, social implications beyond that of the emergence of different patterns in work in industrial society. The main implication is that with the greater differentiation in the nature of work, and the considerable specialization of function which accompanies it, the social world loses what Durkheim describes as its 'organic' solidarity and acquires instead a 'mechanical' solidarity. This theme, of the collapse in industrial society of communities organized around a group of people with interdependent skills is one of the great social themes about the coming of industrialization, and part of what so distressed many nineteenth-century writers (from Nietzsche to William Morris). Different writers had different arguments about this change, and each different writer also had their solution for it, ranging from Nietzsche's valediction of transcendent values to the re-creation of villages in which 'traditional' skills could be practised. About these various attempts to reorder social life and to reverse the passage of time we can note, first, that it was largely in northern, Protestant Europe where this phenomenon was to be found and, second, that such attempts were largely unsuccessful. But what all the attempts are inspired by is a sense of loss, of loss of a past with greater solidarity and one in which human relations are remembered as more cohesive.

The past, as many previous writers have pointed out, is a different country. But the use of the past, and our understanding of it, has very much more than merely academic interest. Writers on industrial society, from Marx onwards, have pointed out that the nature of industrial society can be baffling and mystifying for those who live in it. For Marx, this was related to the fetishism of commodities and human confusion about both the range and the value of goods produced through mechanized production, whereas for others – for example Nietzsche – the confusion is about the values of the society. Throughout the nineteenth century the 'new' industrial society becomes increasingly associated with the ephemeral, the passing and the temporary. Words such as 'fleeting' start to appear in descriptions of urban life and the dominance of fashion becomes a matter of both remark and concern. The French writer Baudelaire (1821–67) is often cited as the first great writer on the 'condition' of life in the modern, urban world. His writings, which appear in the mid-nineteenth century, are much concerned with the ways in which artists can reach significance in the passing and ephemeral world of 'modern', urban life. Baudelaire had a great affection for the Gothic novel, and the appeal of the extra-worldly and the fantastic was of huge appeal to him as a contrast to the tedium of everyday life. In his most famous work *Les Fleurs du mal* (*The Flowers of Evil*, published in 1857), Baudelaire accuses his readers of hypocrisy and smugness. In the preface *Au Lecteur* he writes:

> If rape or arson, poison, or the knife
> Has wove no pleasing patterns in the stuff
> Of this drab canvas we accept as life –
> It is because we are not bold enough![6]

These ideas – about France, the modern and modern culture – belong to the mid-nineteenth century. But by that time moralists were beginning to argue that the 'modern' was essentially amoral and decadent. Again, we can return to Nietzsche for a passionate attack on the values and the preoccupations of the modern world. All modern culture, he wrote,

> requires extreme mannerliness and the newest fashions, inward hasty grasp and exploitation of ephemera, indeed of the momentary: and absolutely nothing else! As a result, it is embodied in the heinous nature of journalists, the slaves of the three M's: of the moment (Moment), of opinions (Meinungen) and of fashions (Moden); and the more an

individual has affinities with this culture the more will they look like journalists.[7]

It is now customary that links are made between Nietzsche and the rise of German fascism, yet much of his writing gives no hint of the connections to come and it is possible to read Nietzsche less as the prophet of Nazism and more as just one of the voices in the nineteenth century concerned with what was seen as the confusion and chaos of the new urban world. In this world, nothing seemed secure or of value: the rate of change and the extent of the new capacities of the world endlessly replaced old certainties and the sense of a secure moral universe. In this context, two issues are perhaps more important than others: first, the question of the extent to which the sense of profound cultural change was general, rather than specific to an educated elite, and second, the way in which many societies and cultures, and not just that of nineteenth-century Europe, create idealized visions of the past, just as much as they have constructed utopian or messianic versions of a world to come. On the first issue we can note that far from fearing change and new forms of social relations, many people and groups in nineteenth-century Europe actively wished for both. For example, in *Jane Eyre*, Charlotte Brontë pleads for a new world for women:

> It is in vain to say human beings ought to be satisfied with tranquillity: they must have action; and they will make it if they cannot find it. Millions are condemned to a stiller doom than mine, and millions are in silent revolt against their lot. Nobody knows how many rebellions besides political rebellions ferment in the masses of life which people earth. Women are supposed to be very calm generally: but women feel just as men feel; they need exercise for their faculties, and a field for their efforts as much as their brothers do; they suffer from too rigid a restraint, too absolute a stagnation, precisely as men would suffer; and it is narrow-minded in their more privileged fellow-creatures to say that they ought to confine themselves to making puddings and knitting stockings, to playing on the piano and embroidering bags. It is thoughtless to condemn them, or laugh at them, if they seek to do more or learn more than custom has pronounced necessary for their sex.[8]

Far from being a condemnation of the modern and of social change, it is a positive plea for it and a passionate critique of all those 'traditional' values which find favour in other quarters. Brontë sees no threat in the coming of a new social order; what she sees is possibility: possibility for human emancipation and the extension of social boundaries. The quotation is perhaps particularly useful and important since it has become so accepted from the nineteenth century onwards to assume that change always has a negative impact and is destructive of established human relationships. What Brontë is arguing is that many existing social relationships are themselves destructive of human beings. When *Jane Eyre* was first published it was regarded in some quarters as a subversive and a seditious book, a novel which constituted nothing less than an attack on the social hierarchy, established religion and the proper ordering of gender relations. It is this kind of reaction – and the lasting vitality of Brontë's plea for changes in the social order – that lends weight to the idea that the coming of change was not universally condemned. Brontë is speaking particularly for women, but other social groups – notably the industrial workforce – might well have agreed with her arguments. It is thus that it is important to recognize the diversity of attitudes to change and the new industrial order in the nineteenth century.

The second issue about change, and perceptions of change, is that for most of history the past has been accorded a positive, and often mythical, status. For centuries, throughout the West, history began in the Garden of Eden, a place from which, according to some interpretations, the world went rather rapidly downhill. This construction of history – that the world began in a place of absolute harmony – is not unique to Christianity, and other religions have also drawn on the idea of human history as a negative departure from a perfect world. But it would seem that this idea is so lodged in the social consciousness of the west that it is sometimes difficult for us to interpret the present without invoking ideas about this lost paradise. Indeed, it is a taken-for-granted premise of sociology, in part derived from the work of Weber, that the modern world has become 'disenchanted'. In *Economy and Society* Weber argued thus:

> As intellectualism suppresses belief in magic, the world's processes become disenchanted, lose their magical significance, and henceforth simply 'are' and 'happen' but no longer signify anything. As a consequence, there is a

growing demand that the world and the total pattern of life be subject to an order that is significant and meaningful.[9]

Read collectively, the views of many nineteenth- and early-twentieth-century writers on the modern world suggest a deep pessimism about its nature and absolute lack of enthusiasm for what some sociologists today are fond of calling the 'project' of modernity. In this we therefore come to one of the many great paradoxes in the history of our understanding of society: at that time, just prior to the First World War, when Europe had been relatively peaceful for almost a century and material life was vastly improving for many citizens, informed and thoughtful critics viewed the world pessimistically. The citizen of Europe in the sixteenth century was used to the idea of random catastrophes, and for many people modern ideas about risk would be nothing compared with the real risks of existence, yet there is little social evidence to suggest that this altogether more perilous society was regarded as 'disenchanted', fleeting or without value. The great tragedies of Shakespeare do not suggest that the social world or human existence is without failure; it is clearly well within the capacity of human beings to make existence miserable but that is to be distinguished from a general sense of the loss of the positive.

The most frequently given explanation for the apparent melancholia that overtook social scientists and other writers on the social world in the nineteenth century is that in this post-Enlightenment period what the world had lost was God, and that without God (by which is generally meant the Christian God), human existence is without meaning because there is no real moral purpose to actions or judgements. Again, our sixteenth-century observer might well query the extent to which God, or the belief in God, was actually a central part of social life in pre-Enlightenment Europe and suggest that many aspects of social life were directed by other kinds of social conventions, customs and superstitions of one kind or another. The historian Keith Thomas, in his definitive study *Religion and the Decline of Magic*, makes the extremely important point that the religious fealty of pre-Reformation Europe has been much exaggerated. He writes:

> The growth of secularism is not a topic which has received much systematic investigation. These authorities who have considered it have tended to pursue the analysis of the

sociologist, Emile Durkheim, to its logical conclusion. If it is by religious ritual that society affirms its collective unity, they argue, then the decline of that ritual reflects the disappearance of that unity. The breakup of shared values, consequent upon the growth of urbanism and industrialism, makes such collective affirmations increasingly difficult. ... This conventional interpretation undoubtedly exaggerates the moral unity of mediaeval society. Durkheim himself romanticized the Middle Ages as a time when men were cosily bound to each other in little units of manor, village and gild; and similar idealization has affected the work of unhistorically minded sociologists.[10]

This argument allows us to explore the possibility that God did not, as Nietzsche famously put it, 'die' in the nineteenth century. Rather, what happened – and what remains central to the twenty-first century – is that new gods appeared, new ideas about the origin of the world and the ways in which it could be made and remade. The Bible and the universe had been undermined by the work of Charles Darwin as the authoritative account of the making of the world. Darwin's work suggested we could understand the evolution of human society; Marx and Engels and working-class and socialist movements of the same period argued that we could choose how the world is run. What Marx and Engels attacked most fundamentally was the idea that the world in which we live is the only way in which the world can be organized. This was not in itself a novel idea, for radical religious sects in the seventeenth century and revolutionaries of 1789 had thought exactly the same thing, but the breadth of the work of Marx was to challenge all assumptions about the 'natural' in the social. If industrialization and urbanization were the two key processes of material transformation in the nineteenth century, then denaturalization was perhaps of the most cultural importance, since it challenged all previous forms of human categorization, in particular those relating to gender and social hierarchy.

The development of the idea of human equality is often associated with the eighteenth century and the emergence of ideas about citizenship. The famous words of the American Declaration of Independence of 1776 (that 'all men are created equal') stand out as the first public declaration that the law of a state should make no distinction between human beings. As has been extensively pointed out, and as we saw earlier in the book, the words 'all men' did, in

1776, mean precisely that: it took some time for the legal status of women to be regarded as a social issue, let alone as a question of the extension of the same rights to women as to men. As has also been pointed out, the words of the Declaration meant everything to white male citizens, very little to those black men and women who remained slaves in the United States until after the end of the American Civil War in 1865. Thus what we can observe in the past four hundred years is that the idea of human equality is not, in its essence, particularly novel, although in its reality it is. But whereas the idea of equality has a long European heritage, what made the implementation of this idea of much more recent realization were ideas about the 'natural' capacities (or lack of them) which were supposed to be possessed by women, children, all members of the working class and people of non-white races. Thus just as Charlotte Brontë speaks passionately for the emancipation of women and the extension to women of the freedoms enjoyed by men, so she makes Jane Eyre speak of the 'coarsely clad little peasants' whom she teaches. But what Brontë also does is remind her readers that these 'little peasants' are of 'flesh and blood as good as the scions of gentlest genealogy'. It is in this latter assertion that we find an example of those powerful ideas which were to inspire social reformers of the nineteenth and twentieth centuries.

Reading the history of eighteenth- and nineteenth-century Europe was, for much of the twentieth century, to read of the relentless progress of human emancipation and the improvement of the lives of ordinary people. A usual pattern of the writing of history other than by Marxist historians, was to suggest that no sooner had a problem been identified – let us say the employment of children in factories in the early years of industrialization – than along came a solution to deal with it, in this case the passing, in Britain, of the Factory Acts. Thus what was presented to students of history, and the history of society, was a narrative of improvement, a narrative tragically interrupted by the First and Second World Wars. Into this account of history came the work of the French historian, Michel Foucault (1926–84), an account of history that was to challenge many of the taken-for-granted assumptions about the process of historical change. It was in the context of the history of mental illness that Foucault was to question much conventional wisdom about social change and in particular the view that the history of knowledge is the history of progress towards the truth. Perhaps most importantly, Foucault does not see the Enlightenment as a movement towards human liberation; unlike the Frankfurt School, Foucault is pessimistic about its lasting values.

The work by Foucault in which he sets out his views on the history of the treatment of the mad is *Madness and Civilization*, originally published in 1961 (although later works, notably *The Birth of the Clinic* (1963) and *Discipline and Punish* (1975) were to take up many of the themes). In *Madness and Civilization* Foucault takes issue with the conventional view that at the end of the eighteenth century there emerged a more humane way of dealing with the 'mad' than that of locking them up. Foucault cites the work done by the Englishman Samuel Tuke, the founder of a 'retreat' for the mentally ill in York. For years the view of Tuke (and others like him who did similar work at the same time in other parts of Europe) was that he was inspired by humane values and that his work could be generally identified with the impact of the Enlightenment on the treatment of the ill and the poor. In this reading Tuke stands in a line with other figures who exemplify eighteenth-century models of improvement, such as the philanthropist Thomas Coram in his work with abandoned children. Foucault, on the other hand, takes a rather different view; he writes that 'Tuke created an asylum where he substituted for the free terror of madness the stifling anguish of responsibility'.

The example of Tuke's methods that Foucault chooses in order to explain his views is that of the tea parties which Tuke held for the inmates of his retreat and invited guests. The point of the tea parties, according to Tuke, was to provide a setting in which the inmates could meet 'ordinary' people and take part in a social occasion in which all participants could treat each other with respect and politeness. According to Foucault, these occasions are not occasions which are helpful to the inmates; on the contrary, he suggests: 'Now the asylum must represent the great continuity of social morality. The values of family and work, all the acknowledged virtues, now reign in the asylum.'[11] What has happened to the mad is that they are imprisoned in a 'moral world'. Foucault was to extend this thesis in other works, but what is crucial to much of his writing is an engagement with the view that the Enlightenment was always a form of human emancipation: for Foucault there was an important sense in which reason, rather than being a force for liberation, is actually an idea through which we are imprisoned. The inmates of Tuke's asylum, who are expected to behave in conventionally appropriate ways at tea parties, are given, in Foucault's account of the world, no place in which to be 'mad', they can only be 'ill' versions of sane human beings. Thus the pre-Enlightenment understanding of 'madness', which was that of a realm of human behaviour and understanding which was generally not available to reason, gave way to a binary distinction between madness and sanity, or reason and absence of reason. Madness as a state of both mind and being was no longer, after the Enlightenment, an option.

The challenge to the orthodoxy of relentless post-Enlightenment progress was Foucault's major challenge to conventional under-standings and accounts of history. On the subject of the treatment of the mad, the criminal and the imprisoned he wrote accounts which took issue with accepted views and suggested instead a reinterpre-tation of the Enlightenment. But what Foucault does not do is to dismiss the idea of reason, and reasoning, which is central to the Enlightenment. His lack of sympathy with the institutional outcome of some of the ideas of the Enlightenment never shifted, but he did not become the spokesperson for 'unreason', which is sometimes suggested. What Foucault remained loyal to was the importance of thinking critically about all existing ideas and assumptions about the world. In the context of all those areas which were the subjects of his work (madness, medicine, sexuality, prisons) there is a consistent refusal to see any category or definition as fixed. For example, Fou-cault, although homosexual himself, was wary of alignment with gay politics: to have done so would have been to accept and live out a created identity which, in his view, did not liberate the individual but locked them into a social definition.

Foucault died in 1984 and by the time of his death had already become an extremely influential figure in the interpretation of both the past and the present. The originality of his work lay less in its emphasis on regulation than on the links that he suggested between knowledge and power: he created a space for the articulation of different 'discourses' which was something of a challenge to those traditions which made much closer links between knowledge and power. Marxism had bequeathed to the understanding of the social world the assumption that ideas are always linked (in more or less complex ways) to the material and economic 'base' of society. Much of academic sociology and history, however formally dismissive of this idea, had done little to challenge this analysis and had implicitly accepted the view that it is the material which determines con-sciousness. Foucault had little interest in the material, and what his work did was to establish a theoretical model in which ideas were primary. But in doing this he has also to be seen as part of a much longer debate about the origins of social actions.

If we return to the beginning of this history – to the world of 1500 – what we find is that explanations of the social world and the actions of human beings are largely limited to explanations drawn from naturalistic explanations about individuals: it is 'natural', it is supposed, for men and women to have certain characteristics associated with their biological sex. Age, gender, race have a direct effect on character and behaviour and the norms which individuals are supposed to follow are drawn from Christian teaching. Literature of the period 1500 to 1700 tells us a great deal about the human capacity for various emotional states and it is recognized that human beings have a considerable capacity for the seven deadly sins of popular parlance. So the individual, and individual behaviour, is considered and various attempts are made to explain the ways in which people act. But the relationship between the social world and individual – and collective – behaviour still has to be explored. That exploration becomes important in the eighteenth century: one of the most important results of the Enlightenment is that it allows the investigation of what has previously been seen as part of the fixed universe; just as the 'natural' world had become the object of scientific enquiry so too would the social world.

Nevertheless, the natural and the social remained, and remain, deeply intertwined and it is this characteristic of European thought which is still part of the twenty-first century. If we look back to the eighteenth century and the work of the Scottish philosopher David Hume we find a mix of radical enquiry and statements of absolute facts about the world. In *Enquiries concerning Human Understanding and concerning the Principles of Morals* (first published in 1777) Hume writes thus of the considerable differences between human beings (all of whom, in this context, are men): 'The difference, which nature has placed between one man and another, is so wide, and this difference is still so much further widened, by education, example and habit . . .'.[12] The important comment here is that it is nature, not the social world, which creates the first differences between people. But even whilst Hume makes this assertion about nature as the origin of human difference he is also capable of social explanation. For example, in considering what he clearly regards as some of the more unfortunate behaviours of the Ancient Greeks, he suggests:

> The Greek loves, I care not to examine more particularly. I
> shall only observe, that, however blameable, they arose from
> a very innocent cause, the frequency of the gymnastic
> exercises among that people; and were recommended,
> though absurdly, as the source of friendship, sympathy,
> mutual attachment, and fidelity; qualities esteemed in all
> nations and ages.[13]

This thesis, that the Greek acceptance of homosexual relationships (the love that Hume does not care to examine 'more particularly') was derived from too much exposure of the body, is
intrinsically modern in the way in which it allows that human
behaviour can be created and that the 'self' is not a stable, fixed
entity. At the same time Hume is still very much a person of the
eighteenth century in that other parts of his work (including that
quoted above) assume 'natural' differences between individuals in a
way which has since become contested. This uneasy and shifting
relationship with 'nature' and the 'natural' in both the human and
the social persists from the eighteenth century to the present day.
Contemporary speech still includes references to the 'natural' and,
although we have come some way to acknowledging that we are
made by circumstance and fortune, there is also a very powerful
sense in which we maintain a belief in the givens of nature. We can
trace the authority of the 'natural' throughout the nineteenth and
twentieth centuries: in the nineteenth century writers whom we now
regard as radical spoke of 'the nature of women' and assumed public
acceptance of givens in human behaviour. In the twentieth century
Freud was to question, and indeed undermine, the idea that human
sexuality developed unproblematically into the masculine and the
feminine but he continued, as many of his critics have energetically
pointed out, to regard 'natural' biological difference as the genesis of
human behaviour.

Yet at the same time as the 'natural' has, in a number of
important ways, remained with us as part of our understanding of
the world, it has also been questioned by two traditions of social
theory. The first is that of Marxism, which challenged the idea that
human society and its values are 'natural' givens. As Marx famously
remarked, the point of understanding society is to change it. This
view, and the politics to which it gave rise, has become part of our
history for the past hundred years; even in those societies which have
not committed themselves to the full implications of Marx's work

there has been a general consensus that the social world can (and often should) be changed. This tradition, of what has become known as 'social engineering', is now an integral part of western politics. The second, and more recent tradition, is that of twentieth-century feminism, which has refused to accept the 'natural' place of women in the world. Recent theoretical work within feminism – for example by Judith Butler – has argued that it is not just theories about the body which are constructed it is also the body itself.[14] In Butler's work we reach the furthest point on the continuum away from nature, and 'natural' explanations, that it has so far been possible for anyone to go: in her view (which follows Freud in its emphasis on the instability of the self) we have to recognize that all our behaviour and all our expectations about the world are socially constructed. There is no 'natural' self, in the sense that this was assumed throughout much of the twentieth century. But if there is no 'natural' self, if we cannot rest securely in the identities of male or female or mother and father, the question that then confronts us is the nature of our modern 'self'.

The making of the modern 'self' has been a subject of concern for writers throughout the twentieth century. The question of how to live is as old as recorded history, but for European writers after the Enlightenment and after the emergence of the dominance of industrial capitalism the matter has taken rather different forms. First, western societies have abandoned the making of civil authority through religion; religion has, although recently articulated through more assertive versions of non-Christian religions, generally given way to more secular values. Second, western societies have given many of their citizens (in most cases about two-thirds) a reasonable material security in which they can pursue their own personal wishes. Legislation about personal life has been both abandoned (for example in the sense that homosexuality has been decriminalized) and increased (for example in the sense that violence and abuse within the home is subject to social control). Thus many of us live in more prosperous worlds than did previous generations and in worlds which are often more formally tolerant. At the same time we are confronted by two powerful themes in writing about the modern self. One is the theme of alienation and anomie, the theme that links the work of writers of fiction (for example, Dostoevsky, Kafka, Camus) with writers about society (Marx, Durkheim, sociologists of 'loneliness' in the United States such as David Riesman and more recently Robert Putnam).[15] The 'lost' person in the modern world is a

recurrent issue. The second is that the modern self has plural identities, of gender, race and class, and that these identities are very far
from being static or constant. These two traditions combine to
communicate a sense of the modern self as an alienated lost person,
trapped in what Baudelaire described as 'this terrible and bleak
tableau'.[16] The individual living in modern Europe shares with the
individual born in the sixteenth century certain characteristics
acquired at birth: a biological sex and a national identity, for example.
But what differentiates the modern self from the sixteenth-century
self is that there is more scope for individual choice in the further
articulation of those characteristics given at birth. A person may
change nationality (or have it changed involuntarily in forced
migration) and make choices about the form and the direction their
sexuality takes. (Contraception made the birth of children a voluntary
part of heterosexuality, for example, just as contemporary gay politics
have made homosexuality a more open and positive social option).
The body can be kept alive longer and indeed modified in various
ways according to the dictates of either personal health or personal
vanity. The birth of children still makes far more impact on the lives
of women than on the lives of men, but other than that the lives of
women and men have achieved a significant degree of similarity.

   Thus the modern self is, in many ways, recognizably more able
to negotiate its personal identity than in the sixteenth century. (It is
worth remembering here that part of the religious settlement of
Elizabeth I was mandatory church attendance.) The Enlightenment
of the seventeenth and eighteenth centuries further extended the
boundaries of what individuals could both know and investigate. Yet
a post-Enlightenment tradition suggests to us that rather than
opening up the world this tradition contributed negatively to its
future. Charles Taylor, in his *Sources of the Self*, writes:

> Thus Enlightenment naturalism thought it was refuting
> Christianity in showing the cost of asceticism; Nietzsche often
> gives a picture of 'morality' which shows it to be merely
> envy, or a device of the weak, or ressentiment, and which
> thus deprives it of all claim in our allegiance. Foucault in
> his writings seems to be claiming (I believe) impossible
> neutrality, which recognised no claims as binding.[17]

What Taylor does here is, in his words, to refute the 'cardinal
mistake of believing that a good must be invalid if it leads to

suffering or destruction'. Taylor in fact defends the values and the ideals of the Enlightenment, not because there is another way of demonstrating that in fact the horrors of the twentieth century had nothing to do with the Enlightenment, but because what he wishes to maintain is a sense of the possibilities which the Enlightenment opened up. In this, he does not adopt a position of pessimism about the modern world, nor does he adopt what he has described, in the context of the work of Foucault, a moral neutralism about the progress of history.

Taylor's work is important as an antidote to much sociological writing about the twentieth and the twenty-first centuries which emphasizes (from Weber onwards) the remorseless progress of bureaucratic industrial capitalism towards a soulless and inherently violent society. Weber himself had written, in *The Protestant Ethic and the Spirit of Capitalism*, that 'The rosy blush of ... the Enlightenment seems also to be irretrievably fading'. Amongst sociologists writing in the late twentieth century the views of Weber remain a powerful influence; there is little general optimism about the nature of the lives of individuals in the contemporary west, except in terms of the greater general material prosperity which technology has made possible. Only Anthony Giddens in *The Transformation of Intimacy* offers a more positive reading of the personal lives of contemporary citizens, a reading which suggests the greater democratization of relations between men and women and a congruent democratization of civil society.[18] Apart from this, there is a more general sense that many of the predictions about the future in George Orwell's novel *1984* have come true: a greater surveillance, a brutal and inane popular culture, a loss of the possibility of political difference, the summary dismissal of history and a negative transformation of language. Orwell's vision of a totalitarian society can be illustrated in many aspects of contemporary culture; indeed Orwell's term 'Big Brother' has itself become part of the culture in which we live.

The fictional totalitarian society which Orwell described in *1984* is often read as an account of Stalin's Russia. But we know that Orwell intended the novel to illustrate totalitarian possibilities in all societies, Europe as much as the Soviet Union. Nietzsche and Weber were the great prophets of this possibility: in their different ways they both suggested the transformation of the social world into a world without values and without a space for what Charles Taylor has described as the 'divine affirmation of the human'. Contemporaries of Weber (for example the political scientist Robert

Michels) underlined the emergent possibilities of totalitarianism in the West. But alongside this tradition we might also set that of Marxism, which identified, as early as the middle of the nineteenth century, the potential richness of the new technological world of capitalism, a richness only made possible through the endless exploitation of those who produced its wealth. Yet what has been added to this equation, and an addition which in itself perhaps bodes well for the future, is concern about the exploitation of nature. The Enlightenment allowed people to use their abilities to control the worst excesses of the natural world; capitalism allowed that ability to be used in endlessly exploitative ways. Nevertheless the very recognition of the finite resources of nature has encouraged the development of thinking which actually brings into concord the natural and the cultural. Old binaries, it would appear, can become less antagonistic. If that is possible, then it may also be the case that some of the divisions which shaped Europe between 1600 and 2000 might become less significant.

Notes and References

Preface

1. Ulrich Beck, *Risk Society: Towards a New Modernity* (London: Sage, 1992); Anthony Giddens, *The Transformation of Intimacy: Sexuality, Love and Eroticism in Modern Societies* (Cambridge: Polity Press, 1992); Donna Haraway, *Simians, Cyborgs and Women: The Reinvention of Nature* (London: Free Association Books, 1991); Bryan Turner, *Body and Society: Explorations in Social Theory* (Oxford: Blackwell, 1984).
2. John Urry, *Sociology Beyond Societies: Mobilities for the Twenty-first Century* (London: Routledge, 2000).
3. Francis Fukuyama, *End of History and the Last Man* (London: Hamish Hamilton, 1992).
4. Patrick Collinson, 'De Republica Anglorum', in Patrick Collinson, *Elizabethan Essays* (London: Hambledon Press, 1994), pp. 1–30.
5. Paul Gilroy, *Black Atlantic: Heterogeneous Culture of Europe* (London: Hutchinson, 1992).

Chapter 1

1. See, for example, the comprehensive study by Olwen Hufton, *The Prospect before Her: A History of Women in Western Europe* (London: HarperCollins, 1995).
2. Diarmaid MacCulloch, *Reformation: Europe's House Divided 1490–1700* (London: Penguin, 2004), p. 73.
3. Walter Benjamin, 'The work of art in the age of technical reproduction', in Hannah Arendt (ed.), *Illuminations* (London: Fontana, 1973), pp. 219–53.
4. Max Weber, *The Protestant Ethic and the Spirit of Capitalism* (London: Allen & Unwin, 1976).
5. The fullest account which Michelet (1798–1874) gives of the Renaissance is in his nineteen volume *Histoire de France*, first published in 1867.

6. Jacob Burckhardt (1818–97), *The Civilization of the Renaissance in Italy*, first published in 1860.
7. Walter Pater (1839–94), *Studies in the History of the Renaissance*, first published in 1873.
8. Johan Huizinga (1872–1945), *The Waning of the Middle Ages*, first published in 1919.
9. Erwin Panofsky (1892–1968), *Studies in Iconology*, first published in 1939.
10. Stephen Greenblatt, *Representing the English Renaissance* (Berkeley: University of California Press, 1988).
11. See Patrick Collinson, *Elizabethan Essays* (London: Hambledon Press, 1994).
12. Weber, *The Protestant Ethic and the Spirit of Capitalism*, p. 104.
13. Ibid., p. 95.
14. Norbert Elias, *The Civilizing Process: Sociogenetic and Psychogenetic Investigations*, Vol.1 *The History of Manners* (New York: Pantheon, 1978), Vol. 2 *State Formation and Civilization* (Oxford: Blackwell, 1982).
15. See Mark Girouard, *Life in the English Country House, A Social and Architectural History* (New Haven, Conn.: Yale University Press, 1978).
16. Weber, *The Protestant Ethic and the Spirit of Capitalism*, p. 49.

Chapter 2

1. Robert Merton, *Science, Technology and Society in Seventeenth Century England* (New York: Harper & Row, 1970).
2. Ibid., p. 110.
3. J. H. Plumb, *England in the Eighteenth Century: 1714–1815* (Harmondsworth: Penguin, 1964), p. 12.
4. Thomas Laqueur, *Making Sex: Body and Gender from the Greeks to Freud* (Cambridge, Mass.: Harvard University Press, 1990).
5. Ernest Gellner, *Encounters with Nationalism* (Oxford: Blackwell, 1994).
6. Jurgen Habermas, *Structural Transformation of the Public Sphere: An Inquiry into a Category of Bourgeois Society* (Cambridge: Polity Press, 1989).
7. Phillipe Aries, *Centuries of Childhood: A Social History of Family Life* (London: Cape, 1962); Lawrence Stone, *Family, Sex and Marriage in England, 1500–1800* (Harmondsworth: Penguin, 1979).

Chapter 3

1. Henry Kamen, *The Iron Century: Social Change in Europe, 1550–1660* (London: Weidenfeld & Nicolson, 1971).
2. Jenny Uglow, *The Lunar Men: The Friends who made the Future* (London: Faber & Faber, 2002).
3. Ibid., p. xiv.
4. E. J. Hobsbawm, *The Age of Revolution, 1789–1848* (New York: Mentor Books, 1962), p. 330.
5. E. P. Thompson, *The Making of the English Working Class* (London: Gollancz, 1963) and Barbara Taylor, *Eve and the New Jerusalem: Socialism and Feminism in the Nineteenth Century* (London: Virago, 1975).
6. Quoted in Jenny Uglow, *Elizabeth Gaskell* (London: Faber & Faber, 1993), p. 140.
7. Elizabeth Gaskell, *Mary Barton* (Harmondsworth: Penguin, 1970), pp. 219–20.
8. R. Hyam, *Empire and Sexuality: The British Experience* (Manchester: Manchester University Press, 1990), p. 60.
9. Karl Marx, *Economic and Philosophical Manuscripts of 1844* (London: Lawrence & Wishart, 1965), p. 98.
10. Karl Marx, *The German Ideology* (London: Lawrence & Wishart, 1963), p. 160.
11. Linda Colley, *Britons: Forging the Nation 1707–1837* (New Haven, Conn.: Yale University Press, 1994).

Chapter 4

1. Hermione Lee, *Virginia Woolf* (London: Vintage, 1996), p. 283.
2. Ibid., p. 278.
3. E. J. Hobsbawm, *The Age of Empire* (London: Abacus, 2003), p. 326.
4. John Maynard Keynes, *The Economic Consequences of the Peace* (New York, Harcourt Brace, 1920)
5. Jill Stephenson, *Women in Nazi Germany* (London: Longman, 2001), p. 55.
6. Elizabeth Wilson, 'Bohemian Love', in Mike Featherstone (ed.), *Love and Eroticism* (London: Sage, 1999), pp. 111–27.

Chapter 5

1. David Cannadine, *The Decline and Fall of the British Aristocracy* (New Haven, Conn.: Yale University Press, 1990).
2. Derek Sayer, *Capitalism and Modernity: An Excursus on Marx and Weber* (London: Routledge, 1991), p. 12.
3. Zygmunt Bauman, *Modernity and the Holocaust* (Cambridge: Polity Press, 1991).
4. Nietzsche, quoted in David Frisby, *Fragments of Modernity* (Cambridge: Polity Press, 1985), pp. 30–1.
5. Walter Benjamin, 'The work of art in the age of mechanical reproduction', in *Illuminations* (London: Fontana, 1970), pp. 219–54 and *The Arcades Project* (Cambridge, Mass.: Belknap Press, 1999).
6. Charles Baudelaire, *The Flowers of Evil* (Oxford: Oxford University Press, 1993), p. 17.
7. Quoted in Frisby, *Fragments of Modernity*, p. 31.
8. Charlotte Brontë, *Jane Eyre* (London: Penguin, 1994), p. 111.
9. Max Weber, *Economy and Society* (Berkeley: University of California Press, 1978), p. 506.
10. Keith Thomas, *Religion and the Decline of Magic* (Harmondsworth: Penguin, 1973), p. 205.
11. Michel Foucault, *Madness and Civilization* (New York: Vintage, 1965), p. 257.
12. David Hume, *Enquiries concerning Human Understanding and concerning the Principle of Morals* (Oxford: Clarendon Press, 2000), p. 170.
13. Ibid., p. 334.
14. Judith Butler, *Gender Trouble* (London: Routledge, 1990).
15. David Riesman, *The Lonely Crowd* (New York: Doubleday, 1953) and Robert Putnam, *Bowling Alone* (New York: Touchstone, 2000).
16. Baudelaire, *The Flowers of Evil*, p. 21.
17. Charles Taylor, *Sources of the Self: The Making of the Modern Identity* (Cambridge: Cambridge University Press, 1994), p. 519.
18. Anthony Giddens, *The Transformation of Intimacy* (Cambridge: Polity Press, 1995).

Index